REFLECTIONS
FROM
PALESTINE

a journey of hope

Samia Nasir Khoury

a memoir

First published in 2014 by
Rimal Publications
Nicosia, Cyprus
www.rimalbooks.com

ISBN: 978-9963-715-11-4

Design: Chara Adamidou

To Yousef
and
To my Parents
Musa and Linda Nasir

Acknowledgements

Ever since Aghavni and Dalia Habash encouraged me to publish my reflections and writings I started wondering whether I actually was up to such a project, and whether they were worth publishing. Thanks to them for sowing those first seeds. My thanks to Rev. Naim Ateek, for taking time to write the foreword. Although short and to the point I know he must have made a special effort. Having worked with him closely for many years as founding members of Sabeel, and a member of the executive board, I know more than anybody else how busy he is. So I am very grateful and honored. My thanks to Ethan Flad for such a beautiful introduction, and for the great opportunity he gave me to post my writings on the Witness on-line magazine when he was its editor many years ago. Without the help and support of Cedar Duaybis, my dear and special friend and colleague at Sabeel, my writings would not have been as meaningful and effective. She is always there for me; a person that I could always rely on for information, language, and integrity. Her prompt feedback helped a great deal in moving ahead quickly with the various chapters. Thanks to my sister Rima, my mentor since childhood for ensuring my politically correct statements. Thanks to my sister–in law Tania for putting soul in some of the family experiences and for checking some details necessary to help the reader understand the context as she read through the script, and to my first grandson Omar, who is always salvaging my work at the computer. And last but not least a special thanks to my daughter Dina who picked me up from the floor after falling off unconscious while working on my computer; for the many hours she took care of me assuring me that I will see my book published, even after I was diagnosed with breast cancer.

This book would have never seen the light without the indispensable help of my editor Morgan Cooper, whom I had met for the first time through our common friends in Hawaii. She was so excited to tell me at the time about the project of teaching writing at Birzeit. It was afterwards when I started working seriously on my book that my sister-in-law Tania recommended her strongly as she experienced her editorial skills through the writing workshops and the writers' festival (Palfest). For the hassle of crossing the Qalandia checkpoint to spend hours with me going through the text thoroughly over and over again, and for her advice and encouragement. I was in for a great surprise when the editor of the publishers Lisa Suheir Majaj turned out to be a relative of my landlord in Jerusalem who I mention in the book. It was a lovely connection and it was a pleasure meeting her in person when she came to Jerusalem for the Mamilla Poetry Festival. I am grateful for her various queries and remarks that helped improve the text. And this paragraph will not be complete without a special thanks to my Publishers Rimal, and Nora Shawwa for making an effort to get the book out in time for my 80th birthday on November 24, 2013 which also coincides with the Sabeel international conference and the celebration of twenty five years of Palestinian Liberation Theology.

Introduction

by Ethan Vesely-Flad

Life under occupation. This is the story that Samia Khoury has told, in poignant and direct prose, for many years on end.

The essays that she wrote over a period of more than five years for the Witness magazine, lift up the perspective of a lifelong educator and a loving family leader – a wife, mother, and grandmother – who is also a voice of radical faith. By describing the minutiae of daily Palestinian existence, Khoury also tells us of the broader socio-political conditions of a people striving to maintain dignity and identity in the face of massive oppression.

Working with Samia as her editor during that period – a time when the hopes of the Oslo Accords had faded into distant memory and a second *Intifada* had sprung up amidst desperation – I always found myself moved by her ability to provide storytelling in the context of insistent, politically pointed commentary. Three chords ring loud and clear through the course of her writing.

First, as Samia reminds us time and again, "The Occupation Is Killing Us All." Only when the Israeli occupation of Palestinian territories ends can we expect to see a true resolution of the conflict. Until that time, our hopes for a lasting peace will be unmet. Despite the Israeli unilateral withdrawal from Gaza in 2005, this hope today seems even more distant and unrealistic – Israeli settlements in the West Bank continue unabated, carving up the land into ever-smaller, isolated, and powerless enclaves.

Second, Samia indicts double standards pronounced by governments, international agencies, and the media. Why is it that the senseless murders of Israelis are cause for public condemnation, but the United States blocks U.N. resolutions that would remand Israel for the death of hundreds of civilians? What is "terrorism" and what is "security," we are asked? What is "justice"? Her narrative proves that those who control the media and military power define our language. We are challenged to face the reality of terms like "collective punishment" in the face of house demolitions, confiscated land, and the blockade of medical supplies resulting in starvation and disease.

Third, we are reminded that personal stories open us to the recognition of common humanity. Presenting herself as a Christian in what is now a majority Muslim and Jewish land, Samia shows that indigenous Palestinians are the "living stones" through which we recognize our faith, making the land of Jesus not only historical text but modern-day parable. We read of gas masks being passed out as the Iraq war begins. Of ten-minute drives that take hours, or never come to their conclusion. Of our author passing out at her computer and awakening in the hospital. Of those whose deaths signify both the failings and possibilities of the peace process – from Edward Said, who she knew personally, to Ahmad El-Khatib, a 12-year-old Palestinian child shot and killed by Israeli forces, whose father was comforted by Zvi Frankental, an Israeli whose own son had been murdered by Hamas. Amidst an occupation that dehumanizes both oppressor and oppressed, Samia provides an incarnational theology that can allow us to see one another in a new light once again.

Samia Khoury's writings speak of dispossession – of land, psychology, and humanity. She asks persistently, "Is anyone listening? Who is speaking out for the Palestinian people?" Yet she also offers a timeless sense of hope: that the experience of a common past tells us that a new day is possible; that nonviolent resistance and a commitment to moral values will lay a foundation for a future in which peoples of diverse religions and ethnicities will live together again in peace in the land we call Holy.

Foreword

It was my pleasure to welcome the audience at Sabeel Ecumenical Liberation Theology Centre in Jerusalem for the launching of Samia's book "A Rhyme for Every Time." And when I said it was Samia's first book, she commented that it was her only book. It was a light read written from the heart for family and friends on various occasions. However she surprised us two years later with this book also written from the heart, but is certainly not a light read as she writes about the long years of a military occupation. Her style and language flow simply and easily as she reflects on the daily events and tries to analyze what is really happening. She makes her reader live with her the anxiety of a mother and grandmother, yet she never sounds bitter and never loses hope because she strongly believes in the justice of the cause of her people, the Palestinians.

Rev. Naim Ateek
Founder and Director
Sabeel Ecumenical Liberation Theology Centre
Jerusalem

Preface

I am writing this on the eighth anniversary of the passing away of Yousef, my husband of forty four years; years filled with love, compassion and cooperation in bringing up and caring for the children, as well as the grandchildren. With patience and understanding he coped with my long hours of volunteer work, especially at the YWCA (Young Women's Christian Association) after 1967 when the need to serve the community was so pressing. He always enjoyed quoting the well known alternative meaning of the YWCA "Your Wife Constantly Away." I do not think I could have done or achieved what I did during those long years without his support, and that of my mother, who very often looked after the children especially when I had to travel. My volunteer work was not limited to the the YWCA, but also Birzeit University, Rawdat El-Zuhur and Sabeel Ecumenical Liberation Theology Centre. Very often Yousef also volunteered his engineering services to some of the organizations I was involved with. He was the chairman of the Arab Housing Society which provided housing for many families in Beit Hanina and Ramallah. And for many years he served on the Justice and Peace Commission of the Catholic Church, but unfortunately he passed away on April 10, 2004 without realizing his dream of either justice or peace.

At the time when the second *Intifada* (popular uprising) erupted in the Palestinian Territories, after the provocative visit of Prime Minister Sharon to Al-Aqsa mosque on September 28, 2000, I was getting hooked on technology and communication via e-mail.

Although I learned how to type as early as the summer of 1947 at the YMCA evening school in West Jerusalem, and I brushed up my skills during my years at Southwestern University, I had to take a computer course at the YWCA of Jerusalem. That is when I started sharing my reflections and stories of what was happening, which never seemed to reach beyond our local papers. Some of my contacts had no clue what life under a military occupation was like. As I got responses to my e-mails, I was surprised to find out how widely my messages were being circulated, and how greatly appreciated they were.

Sister Dorothy wrote: "Samia, are the e-mails that you send written by you? If so you must be a reporter or a correspondent." Well being neither one, I was still encouraged, especially when Roula wrote to say that it was precisely the personal nature of my messages that make them so suitable to share; "they strike a deep chord, and many of my friends are now addicted to your weekly updates." Our friends the Reids* from Australia wrote to say: "Day by day the international news media brings us stories of your suffering yet it is nothing compared with the stories you have so kindly sent us during the year of the real situation on the ground." And Samar wanted me to have her new e-mail address because she found my messages very inspiring as they kept her connected with real events that were occurring in her homeland. From Sweden Kerstin who had been to Jerusalem wrote to say that she does not know how I could still smile and have hope living in such a terrible situation. And Huda thought I was a 'whiff of fresh air". Of course I was humbled by those messages because I felt they were genuine, and thanks to them I was encouraged to continue sharing my stories and reflections.

My list was getting longer and wider reaching out to different geographic locations. Ethan Flad, the editor of the Witness magazine at that time, whom I had met through Sabeel was on that list and he asked me to contribute an article regularly to the on-line Witness magazine, an Episcopalian publication. Although I was apprehensive at the beginning, my friend Cedar Duaybis assured me that so long the occupation prevails, there will always be something to inspire me for my monthly essay. I wrote for a period of almost five years until the magazine ceased to be published in 2006 for financial constraints. The first posting in September 2001 was a dialogue with an Israeli woman, Terry Greenblat who was director of Bat Shalom, a national Israeli women's peace organization, and it was facilitated by Gina Benevento. My last article "Still hoping for an honest broker" was posted in the last issue of the Witness on November 9, 2006, and six years later, we are still hoping for an honest broker. In fact as I was collecting my writings for this book, I sadly realized that some of those articles written as far back as 2004 are still as pertinent in 2012. All my 36 articles written for the Witness are saved on my blog http://samiakhoury.wordpress.com/

Samia Khoury
Jerusalem, 2013

*Both Janet and Alan Reid from Australia passed away

A New Reality Overnight

My father sounded very serious as he spoke to me on the phone that morning of June 5, 1967. "Bring the children and come stay with us; it will be safer for all of you in Birzeit than near the military camp where you are."

Yousef and I had been living in our new home in Beit Hanina (a suburb north of Jerusalem, midway to Ramallah) since 1964. There was a Jordanian military camp right behind our house. My father was right that Birzeit was safer—but neither he nor the Israeli pilots raiding the area realized that the military camp had been evacuated before the 1967 war had even begun.

As I hung up the phone, the first question that came to my mind was whether this would be the beginning of another *Nakba*. Although almost twenty years had passed, the memory of the 1948 *Nakba*, when hundreds of thousands of Palestinians had been forced from their homes, fleeing at gunpoint or out of fear, was still potent. What if, like them, I could not return to my home after fleeing? So many cherished memories were lost, so many treasured belongings of entire families. The dispossession was not only of land, but also of identity. My parents, my aunts and uncles, and my father's cousins who were living in West Jerusalem and Jaffa at the time had all suffered in the *Nakba*.

In the aftermath of 1948, when the state of Israel was created on Palestinian land, the Palestinian territories that did not fall into Israeli hands were disconnected from one another. The area on the west bank of the river Jordan, including East Jerusalem, was annexed to Jordan, while the Gaza Strip came under the administration of Egypt, the country with which it shared a border.

I had to think very quickly about what to take with me. I definitely knew that I could not bear to lose the family photo albums and the collection of slides Yousef had taken of the children. All else could be replaced, but a childhood could not be relived.

The yellow canary with his beautiful song seemed to sense the tension in the air. I set the cage near the albums to assure the small bird that we were not abandoning it, and continued packing. It was only at the last minute that I realized that my husband would not be coming with us. He had agreed to serve with the civil guard for our area, and was determined to stay put. I could not envisage how he was going to be of any help as a civil guard when he had not even been given a baton, let alone a gun. But knowing Yousef, I did not argue any further. He spared me carrying the albums, the slides and the canary cage.

What a different day it was from the previous day, when we had all been at the Church of the Gallilia on the Mt. of Olives attending the wedding of Yousef's sister, Wilhelmine, to my cousin, George Baramki. After the wedding everyone gathered at our house for a beautiful reception. The Farradj cousins from Amman joined us for the occasion. They were anxious to go back that same evening, however, because tension was mounting, and fear of an imminent war was acute. The day before the wedding, when we all went to church for the rehearsal, the Mt. of Olives had been filled with Jordanian soldiers. But on the wedding day there wasn't one soldier around; it was too quiet, almost eerie.

The drums of war had been beating ever since Egypt, under the rule of President Jamal Abdel Nasser, decided to end the mandate

Wedding reception of George Baramki & Wilhelmine Khoury at our house

of the United Nations Emergency Forces (UNEF) stationed on the Sinai Peninsula after the 1956 war. These forces had served to guarantee access to Israel through the Straits of Tiran that were under Egyptian sovereignty. Israel considered the closure of the Straits to those vessels sailing to its port a provocation and a call to war. In the meantime, Jordan's King Hussein had flown to Egypt at the end of May 1967 and signed a defense pact with Egypt, under which Jordan joined the Egyptian-Syrian military alliance of 1966 and placed its army under Egyptian command. But Israel took everybody by surprise on the morning of June 5, 1967 when it launched a preemptive strike that grounded the Egyptian air force before it could initiate or respond to any attack. Israel proceeded in a few short days to win the war on all three fronts, occupying the West Bank and Gaza as well as the Sinai and the Golan Heights.

Resigned and heavy-hearted, I left with the children to Birzeit. Soon enough Yousef realized that the Jordanian military camp behind our house had already been evacuated, except for two Jordanian soldiers who were keeping the Israeli planes busy by shooting at them as they flew back and forth over the area. Yousef offered to make the soldiers some tea with mint, but when he went back with the tea, the soldiers had disappeared. I suppose they realized that the game was over; they could no longer keep up the pretext of an entire battalion.

The war was on. One of the bombs dropped by the planes fell directly on the strawberry bed in our garden, breaking our living room window. This gave the Israeli soldiers who went later to investigate the battle scene easy access to our house. They plundered the few small silver items that we had in the living room, as well as the silver cutlery that had been left on the table after the wedding reception the day before. Whoever stole those items must have been either a collector or a silversmith, because he did not touch anything else. Not that I was a collector myself, but those items were meaningful to us because they were wedding gifts from special friends seven years earlier. It was a blessing that Yousef did not hear the thieves from the bedroom at the other end of the house, for no silver would have been worth his life.

We had not been prepared for war; nor were we prepared for occupation. It was a completely humiliating and traumatic experience for all Palestinians. We ourselves felt the trauma acutely as we gathered in the family house.

Our house was located on the premises of Birzeit College. The college had been founded as a school in 1924 by my late aunt Nabiha Nasir and her teacher Ratibeh Shuqair, using my grandfather's summerhouse for the purpose. My father's family is from Birzeit, and my grandfather, Rev. Hanna Nasir, was an Anglican pastor who served in different parts of Palestine. When he retired, he and my grandmother lived in the family quarters within the school. In the early fifties, after the passing of aunt Nabiha in 1951, my father,

Musa Nasir, started developing the school into a junior college. By June 1967 the last class of high school seniors were taking their final exams, and in the fall of 1967 Birzeit became exclusively a junior college.

Almost over night the whole population of the west bank of Jordan and the Gaza Strip found themselves facing a new reality – a military occupation. It took us a while to overcome the shock. When Yousef followed us to Birzeit the next day and saw so many cars along the way crushed by military tanks, he broke the news to us that the Israeli army was on its way. Jerusalem had been captured, and the Israeli Military Forces were marching through the rest of the West Bank. The students trapped in Birzeit because of the war did not believe him, especially since they were all listening to radio broadcasts by the Jordanian monarch assuring us that all was well and that we should hold on and resist by all means. The king probably meant that we should hold on by our bare hands, or even our fingernails, as he had suggested. After all, the whole population was unarmed. Under Jordanian rule nobody had ever been allowed to own guns other than hunting rifles, which needed special permits. Some people who were killed on the roads had actually been outside to welcome the tanks, mistaking them for Arab Forces coming to our rescue. How Yousef survived the risky drive from Beit Hanina to Birzeit and back to Beit Hanina the next morning was beyond me. But that was my Yousef. He was adventurous, and never waited for things to come to him. He always took the initiative to seek things out, and was always excited to be involved when there was action. The more I thought about it, the more I realized it was a real miracle that he had survived.

In the meantime, some of the townspeople came to consult with my father, who was a town elder, a politician and an educator. They wanted to know whether they should leave before it was too late. My father advised everybody to stay put even if it meant facing the Israeli army.

However, some Jordanian soldiers who were abandoned by their units were very worried about surrendering, so they tried to get rid of their uniforms and find refuge in civilian homes. Yousef's uncle Victor, who was living alone in Jerusalem in the Sheikh Jarrah quarter, hosted one of those soldiers. At first he was hesitant to open the door to the very loud and desperate knock, but when he finally realized who the late intruder was, he immediately allowed him in and gave him a pair of pajamas to replace his uniform. Victor thought the wisest thing to do was to remove any traces of the soldier having been there by burning all his gear. So he dumped everything, including the boots, into the bathroom water-heating burner, a common household fixture known as a "geezer." He was in for a surprise when the bullets, which he had not realized were part of the gear, started to explode in the burner. It sounded very funny later, when he shared that unique experience with us, but it certainly was not funny at the time. He had the scare of his life, thinking for sure that the sound of the explosion could easily be heard outside the house.

For us as a family, Birzeit, both the town and the school, had always been the center of our lives. Although we had lived in different parts of Palestine over the years, my siblings, cousins and I spent most of the year at the school in Birzeit as boarders. Even during the summer holidays we would still spend a month there during the grape-harvesting season. The walk to the vineyards in the early morning, known as sarhah, with our snack of ziwadeh— freshly baked whole wheat bread and goat's milk cheese—was a real treat. Once in the vineyards, we could pick grapes and eat them right off the vine, for they grew naturally, without any pesticides. In our younger years, when the walk was too far for our tiny feet, we would ride the donkey that was part of the school landscape. Its caretaker, Shura'a, would load it almost daily with gallons of drinking water from the nearby fresh-water springs. After we graduated from university in 1954, my sister Rima and I returned to work at Birzeit as it was developing into a junior college. My brother Hanna joined us a couple of years later after he graduated from the American University of Beirut.

Those memories were to be forever marred by the events of June 1967. The innocent days of childhood and young adulthood were gone for good.

As the war broke on June 5, my sister, my sister-in-law Tania, and I huddled with our children in an underground storeroom upon the instructions of my father. Our husbands were not with us. Rima's husband, Dr. Antone Tarazi, was stationed at the Jordanian military hospital in El-Bireh near Ramallah, and my brother, Hanna, was still studying in the States. My father insisted that the basement would be the safest place for the children. Meanwhile, my parents and aunts and the family of my sister-in-law took refuge on the upper floor. Tania's uncle, Alex Dabbas, who had fled from Jaffa in 1948 and since then had taken refuge in Egypt, was visiting Tania's family at the time. He joined us in Birzeit as well. As tensions mounted, his sense of humor and his Egyptian accent proved to be the best therapy for us all. Afterwards, it took us a while to stop associating the smell of garlic and onions hanging in the storeroom with that nightmarish experience.

Forty-eight hours after the war had started, the Israeli army was driving through Birzeit calling on everybody to surrender. We used one of the diapers of baby Musa, my brother's son, as a white flag of surrender. Tania, the baby's mother, took upon herself the task of hanging it on a pole from the veranda. It was utterly humiliating. My father almost collapsed at the thought of the Israeli army walking freely in our streets without meeting the slightest resistance. As the Israelis drove by the men's college dorm, they spotted the pile of mattresses stacked away for the summer holiday through the windows, and mistook them for a barricade. They started shooting, and the mattresses caught fire. My mother was absolutely traumatized as she and the staff ran to the place and tried to extinguish the fire and clean up the resulting mess.

Birzeit College had always been very important to my mother. Ever since my parents had been forced to leave their home in West Jerusalem in 1948 and had come to live in Birzeit, she, like the rest of the family, had become deeply involved in the College. She took on the task of supervising housekeeping and food services, and the students vouched that she really made a difference in the quality of those services. She was dedicated and compassionate, and cared about the welfare of the students as if they were her own children. She was particularly worried about the safety and needs of those students who could not go home on the day the war started, and who were therefore stranded at the school.

At the time, there was no electricity in Birzeit. Only the College had a private generator, installed in the 1950s after all of us, my siblings and first cousins, had graduated from high school. The generator would run for a few hours only in the evenings. Around 9:45 p.m. the maintenance man would turn it on and off a few times to signal that it was going to be turned off completely at 10:00 p.m. Turning off the generator, however, never deterred us from staying up late. At the signal, we would simply prepare the kerosene lamps to enable us to finish our work, or the monopoly and lexicon games we used to play. But the night the Israeli army entered Birzeit they took over the generator as well as the men's dorm.

It was the generator that later that summer alerted us to the Israeli army's departure. When, around the middle of June, we heard the generator running at 3:00 a.m., we realized that the army was pulling out of the dorm and the town. What a relief! My mother was very anxious to visit the dorm to assess the condition in which it had been left. First thing in the morning she took a cleaning crew with her. Just then, however, an Israeli army officer showed up to pick up something he had forgotten in the building. When he left, my mother noticed that he had a gun in his hand. Fortunately, nobody had returned to the building earlier and stumbled upon that gun. She did not want to even think of the repercussions that would have ensued had a member of the staff or a student been found with that gun before the officer retrieved it. Under a law imposed by the British Mandate, which Israel saw very fitting to apply, blowing up an entire building was a normal procedure when arms were found in any building.

When the army evacuated the dorm and that first nightmare ended, we were left in shock. We could not believe what had actually happened, especially as we had been listening for more than a week to so much encouraging rhetoric on the Arab Radio stations. Moreover, the surprise visit of King Hussein to Egypt shortly before the war, on May 30, to sign up with the Joint Arab Forces, had left us feeling assured that all would be well and that victory was imminent. The disappointment was just as great for us as it was for those Palestinians who had managed to stay in historic Palestine after Israel was established. It was only after the Israelis evacuated from Birzeit that many of us realized that the November 1966 invasion of Sammu', in the Hebron area, when the Israeli army walked through the town and left it at the end of the day, might have been a rehearsal for the June war. No wonder our anger at that time was actually more focused on the Arab armies who had lost the war on three fronts than on the Israelis. The hope that an Arab Alliance would be our salvation had been completely shattered.

Eventually, on the 19th of June, when everything had settled down, I packed up the children and drove home to Beit Hanina. I remember the date specifically because it was the birthday of Tania, my sister-in-law. We were so happy to be back home and reunited with Yousef. His sister, Lucy, who had come from Rome for the wedding of her sister, was staying with him. During that period, Lucy was working at the Jordanian Embassy in Rome. Her return to work caused a political crisis, as she had to have an Israeli exit stamp on her Jordanian diplomatic passport: there was no other way for her to go back to Rome except via the Lod (Ben Gurion) airport, which Jordan considered an enemy airport at that time.

Once home, I learned that one of the victims of the war was our dog "Damascus." She had been named Damascus by a friend who found her at Damascus Gate in Jerusalem. Our friend could not keep her, as she was staying at the American Colony Hotel. She was very happy to find a home for Damascus on our property with Abed, the young man who was working for us and living in a small cottage in the garden with his wife and baby girl. But Abed and his family had to leave Damascus behind when they ran away to Jericho during the war. I suppose Damascus felt abandoned and took to the main road. One of our neighbors saw a car run her down there. We had to feed her puppies with bottles of milk until we found homes for them, except for the one that we adopted.

Luckily, by the time we arrived in Beit Hanina the electricity was on. It had apparently been cut off, and everything in the freezer had thawed. Not even the cats were willing to eat that food. What a waste, I thought, when there was so much need. We did not realize how fortunate we were to get our electricity back earlier than some other areas, until one morning when the Apostolic Delegate Msgr. Sepinski, whose residence was on the Mt. of Olives, rang our door bell, seeking our service to use his electric shaver. Yousef had been the engineer of the Delegation for many years, and it was the least we could do to help. During such times one realizes that people may be better off when they are not so dependent on technology.

Today such a thought would be blasphemy. I, for one, cannot imagine how I used to type and retype documents for my father who never rushed into sending a letter or a report until he had time to read it again and again, and make changes to draft after draft.

One of the first measures Israel took during those early days of the occupation was to collect all the arms that people owned. The population was given instructions and deadlines for handing in their arms. Of course, in the West Bank the only weapons people had were hunting rifles, but in the Gaza strip there were plenty of arms, because a lot of the resistance movement was in that part of Palestine. Another devious measure which people were tricked into was an order to exchange all Jordanian money or hard currency for Israeli shekels. Unfortunately many people fell in the trap. I remember my husband becoming extremely upset with his father for obeying such orders without challenging them or consulting with his own family. Personally we had no problem, as the only cash we had on us was around one hundred dinars, which I had withdrawn from the bank the day before the war. But as the banks stayed closed it became clear that one hundred dinars were not going to keep us going for long. So we decided to sell my car for cash. Although eventually the sale did not go through, as the buyer did not have cash either, I was almost in tears when Yousef drove the car that morning to deliver it. I needed that car badly, because Beit Hanina at that time lacked basic transportation facilities. More than that, it had been my birthday gift that year.

My mother with my brother's children infront of her father's house in Jaffa

A Brief "Honeymoon"

At the beginning of the occupation, nobody envisioned how long it would last. We were all sure that the international community would not allow the seizure of land by force, and that no occupation would be viable in the 20th century. How naive we were! We refused to think otherwise, despite our frustrating experiences from 1948 onwards, including all the unimplemented United Nations' resolutions on Palestine. Of particular importance to Palestinians everywhere was the General Assembly Resolution 194, a resolution for which the United States had voted, pertaining to the right of return of the Palestinian refugees. The right of return is an individual and collective right enshrined in the Universal Declaration of Human Rights Article 13 (2). But in all those years since 1948, the Palestinian right of return had not been implemented.

Meanwhile, the reality began to sink in. While Israel kept boasting of "the benevolent occupation," the Palestinians who in 1948 had become second class Israeli citizens overnight, and with whom we had connected again at last, assured us that we were still in the "honeymoon period." They had gone through it all before us. It was only in 1966, for instance, that they stopped needing permits to travel internally from one town to another.

In the meantime, we seized the opportunity of this "honeymoon period" to visit pre-1948 Palestine for the first time since the *Nakba*. Ironically, it was only under occupation that we were allowed access to pre-1948 Palestine again, and were able to fulfill the dream of visiting the homes we had been forced to abandon in the 1948 war, and which we had been prohibited from returning to.

Visiting homes lost in the *Nakba* was the very first thing that most families did, some were welcomed by the new Jewish residents who had settled in their homes, and were allowed to look around, while others were not allowed to even come close to their homes. Still others just stood there, recollecting beautiful memories and refusing to go in, so as not to see the present condition of their once-upon-a-time-home. Some found creative ways of entering as Mrs. Aniseh Odeh, who with her fair looks and blue eyes did not look typically Palestinian, was allowed into the house she and her family owned until 1948 when she asked permission to use the rest room. The new Israeli owner was taken by surprise as she watched Aniseh heading straight to the bathroom without waiting for directions. My father-in-law found four families in his house—immigrants from other Arab countries. They invited him in and offered him a soft drink. We even heard stories of people who had hidden their jewelry in the garden of their homes before they left in 1948 and who actually found it upon returning. There were endless stories, and endless emotions.

My mother had a different experience when she visited her parents' home in Jaffa. Finding many changes, she actually started advising the new residents on how to arrange the house so as to better accommodate the families living there! How typical of my mother, I thought. I could not tolerate the idea that she was really advising them—the intruders, the usurpers—on how to make her father's home more comfortable for them. But then that was my mother. She was always a caring person, and wanted the best for everybody. However, she did not have much to say when we visited our own home in Upper Baka'a in West Jerusalem. It had been turned into a clinic, and we did not need to ring the bell. We simply walked through, had a look and before leaving made it a point to tell the receptionist, who saw us walking through, that it was our home.

With the Jordanian license plates still on our car—later all license plates were changed to Israeli plates with different codes for each occupied area—my husband and I drove to visit his home in Lower Baka'a. However, we did not try to go in. We were surprised to realize how close our homes were to each other: we had never met during that period, and our families did not know each other until later in the fifties, when my cousin Laura Baramki married Yousef's brother, Dr. Abdallah Khoury. Ironically, neither Yousef nor I were at their wedding in 1956. Yousef was still in the USA, and I was in Egypt playing table tennis with the Jordanian team in a pan Arab tournament.

Both Palestinians who had remained in what became Israel as well as Jewish families looked up Palestinian friends living in the now Occupied Territories. Connecting with old friends under such circumstances was truly a bitter-sweet encounter. Even when we took the children to the Sea of Galilee and the beach of Jaffa to relive with them our own childhood, the experience was very painful. I could not stop crying as I sat reminiscing over the loss of our country. The Grand Hotel in Ramallah, known to many as "Hotel Audeh," was seized for a while by the Israeli military, and served as temporary headquarters after the June 1967 war. Eventually, however, it became a great meeting place for reunions between Palestinians on both sides of the country. It was a resort hotel familiar to many people who had originally lived in the coastal areas of Palestine and who used to come to Ramallah for summer holidays. For my generation, it had been our only outlet after we all returned from university in the fifties. We had danced till the early hours of the morning to the melodies of beautiful Italian and Spanish bands that came especially for the summer months. All that ended with the occupation. Aida

Audeh, the owner and a beautiful hostess, eventually closed the place up as a hotel, although she continued to live there for many years until she passed away in September 2012.

One memorable encounter was when the Eizenbergs, our Jewish neighbors of bygone years in Safad, came to visit my parents in Birzeit weeks after the occupation. Their daughter, Batia, who was around my age, came with them. I would have loved to see them, but I was already living in Beit Hanina. Mrs. Eizenberg and my mother had been very close and used to exchange treats on Jewish and Christian holidays. Their friendship actually went even further than that. Mrs. Eizenberg would have been willing to entrust her daughter to my mother had the Germans won the Second World War. When my mother passed away, in 1986, I found Batia's address amongst her papers. My first reaction was to think, "how nice, I can now reconnect with her." But the more I thought about it, and thought about how entrenched the occupation had become, the more I hesitated. I eventually did drop her a note to rekindle our acquaintance, but the letter came back undelivered. It was not meant for us to meet again. Perhaps we were thus spared the pain of losing those beautiful memories of years gone by.

We soon started to realize what the Palestinians of Israel were talking about when they told us that we were still in the "honeymoon" period. How right they were, for there is no such thing as a benevolent occupation; occupation is occupation. It is a process of dehumanization and deprivation of freedom of all basic rights.

I had my first personal taste of this dehumanization at the entrance of Dahyiet El-Barid neighborhood about one kilometer north of our house, a neighborhood that forty-one years later became isolated behind the infamous wall. On that morning in late September 1967, after the children had gone off to the Rosary Sisters Kindergarten, I got a call from my sister-in-law, Laura, asking for my help, as she had a terrible back-ache and could not move. I spent the morning with her in Dahyiet el Barid neighborhood, where they were living in a rented house before they moved to their own home in our neighborhood in 1977. Around noon, when it was time for my children to come home, I excused myself and left. To my horror, as soon as I reached the end of the street before the main road, I was stopped by soldiers who ordered me at gunpoint to go back from where I had come. I insisted that I had come from my house a few hours ago, and that I needed to return there, because I was expecting the school bus to drop my children off at home shortly. The soldiers told me that the whole neighborhood was under curfew and that I was not supposed to be driving there. When I challenged them, saying that I had come through in the morning and that they could not impose a curfew without prior announcement, they insisted that there had been an announcement the day before that Ramallah would be under curfew. I again argued with them, saying that they needed a lesson in geography, because Dahyiet el-Barid was not in Ramallah. At that point they did not have any more patience for my cynical comments and threatened to shoot if I did not turn back. Irja' (go back), one of them started screaming. It was then that I really became petrified. I returned to my sister-in-law shaking, with tears in my eyes, worried above all that the children would come home and not find anybody. Seeing those trigger-happy young soldiers, I had no alternative but to obey orders; otherwise the children would lose me forever. I was eventually saved by the school bus that dropped off Laura's younger girls. Leaving my car behind, I stretched out in the bus under the legs of the teachers who were accompanying the children, and was successfully smuggled out of the area. Luckily, I found when I returned home that Yousef had come home earlier than expected and was there for the children. Never have I felt more grateful to be back home than at that moment.

That incident brought back memories of April 22, 1963, when I was pregnant with my second child and was living in the Majaj apartment in Jerusalem. High school students in Jerusalem (part of

Jordan at that time) were peacefully demonstrating, rejoicing at the talks being led by Jamal Abdel Nasser for Egyptian, Syrian and Iraqi unity. I decided to go visit my cousin Laurice in order to watch what was going on, leaving my two-year old daughter in the care of my house helper. I had hardly reached Laurice's house around the corner when shooting started and everybody ran to take shelter. The demonstrators had a confrontation with the Governor of Jerusalem, and in no time the Jordanian Army Special Forces (El-Badiyeh) crashed the demonstration and hell broke loose. Many from the Mamounieh Girls' School, which was close to my cousin's house, took shelter behind the wall in Laurice's garden. There I was, stuck at Laurice's house with my bulging belly, due to have my baby any time. My hair dresser, Leon, who had seen me passing by earlier, was shocked that I would be on the street on such a day, and advised me to go back home. As I was only a few steps away from Laurice's home, I assured him it would be all right. But it certainly was not all right.

Eventually, when all was quiet and the streets were empty, following the imposition of a curfew, my cousin went out and asked the soldiers who were monitoring her street to allow me to go home. I could hear the echo of my footsteps on the street. It felt very strange being the only one walking on the street while snipers patrolled the area from the tops of buildings. Yousef's office was in the Ma'atouk building, across the street from the National Palace Hotel, and he was watching the street closely as I walked towards home. He did not dare take the chance of either waving to me or coming out to walk me home. I kissed the floor when I arrived home, and picked up Dina and hugged her dearly in a way that made her wonder what was going on. That same evening I was rushed to St. Joseph's hospital to deliver my son Suhail.

Beginning of the Nightmare

Along with the "honeymoon" went Israel's euphoria of victory. Eventually, we became numbers on identity cards, carrying bundles of documents and permits for moving, traveling, or uniting with our families. East Jerusalem had been annexed on the 27th of June, shortly after the war was over, and Israel started imposing municipal taxes. Initially we all refused to pay these taxes, because taxation of occupied territories is illegal under international law. In no time the police started confiscating merchandise from stores and furniture from the homes of people who would not comply. The population gave in and started to pay. As in every occupation, Israel actually employed Palestinians to do this dirty job, and those people were considered collaborators. It was not much different from the days of Jesus Christ under the Roman occupation. According to Luke 18:13, the tax collector did repent and admitted that he was a sinner – which was very similar to what many Palestinian collaborators did later on.

I remember one of those Palestinian tax collectors who came to our door and asked for the Arnona, the Hebrew word for municipal tax. I argued with him that he was not entitled to it, but he threatened to call the police. So I promised him to pay by

From right: Amin Nasir, Kamal, Rima and Yousef Batrouni

Kamal at the Jordan Parliament

installments, thinking that maybe the occupation would soon come to an end. When he came the next day to collect the first installment I gave him fifty shekels. "Are you making fun of me?" he questioned. I responded that I wasn't, and that he had never said there was a minimum amount for the installment. He did summon the police, but I succeeded in proving to them that he was not telling the truth when he reported that I refused to pay. I did not understand one word of what the police told him, but I figured from their tone that they were rebuking him as they drove off. That was the last time he came to our house. However, we all caved in eventually, and started paying. As an occupied population we had no backing, neither from world opinion nor the United Nations, to see that international law was applied.

In no time, violations of human rights marked every town, every family and every organization. But the Palestinian population refused to make it easy for Israel to continue occupying the areas. The resistance reached its climax with the *Intifada*, the popular uprising against Israeli occupation that began in December 1987.

But we as a family had our share of that suffering long before the *Intifada* began. One of our most terrible family tragedies resulting from the occupation concerned my cousin, Kamal Nasir. Kamal was assassinated in Beirut in April 1973, along with two other PLO leaders, Yousef el-Najjar and Kamal Adwan, by an Israeli hit squad led by Ehud Barak. The PLO had been established in 1964 after the Palestinians had given up on believing that the United Nations would redress the injustice that was inflicted on the Palestinians in 1948 or that it would implement the many United Nations resolutions pertaining to the rights of the Palestinians. (Although the charter of the PLO called for armed struggle to liberate all Palestine, this was amended after the signing of the Declaration of Principles between the PLO and Israel in 1993. However, some PLO factions, as well as some Palestinians in the Diaspora, did not think the amendment was constitutionally valid.)

Kamal had not been a combatant: he was a poet and a writer. But his literary talents were leavened by activism. Many of Kamal's poems were put to music by my sister Rima Nasir Tarazi, my cousin Amin Nasir, and maestro Yousef Batrouni, and were used as national anthems. In the fifties and sixties, Kamals' poems were sung by the choir of Birzeit College. These poems were very popular, and became part of the movement for liberation and freedom from colonial rule in the area.

Kamal had lived in exile for many years during the Jordanian rule of the West Bank, but had returned to Birzeit shortly before June 1967, when Jordan declared a general amnesty for political prisoners. For quite some time during the Jordanian rule of the West Bank he had been on the run, accompanied by an elder from our hamouleh (clan) as he moved from village to village and from hiding place to hiding place.We hardly recognized him when, masked under a hattah and I'qal and wearing a Qumbaz (traditional dress for men in villages), he came to visit my father one evening. He eventually settled down in the attic of his parents' house in Birzeit. But one day, as he was coming downstairs to see his mother, he realized he had been spotted by one of Jordan's secret service men. He immediately got a cousin to drive him to Nablus, where he stayed with his sister and her husband. While in Nablus, he developed a special relationship with his three-year old nephew, Maher, who was smart enough not to divulge the secret hiding place of his uncle. However, concealing Kamal was not an easy task for his sister nor for her husband, who was the pastor of the Anglican parish in Nablus and whose home was always open to guests. It was after he was deported that he became the spokesman for the Palestine Liberation Organization (PLO) in Lebanon. It was because of Kamal's writings and his speeches that he was targeted by the Israeli hit squad that took his life.

Despite the great tragedy of Kamal's assassination, we can never think of him without remembering the many adventures and funny episodes of his life. Until that fatal night of April 10, 1973, he had escaped arrest time after time. Under Israeli occupation, Kamal had been one of the first to be deported out of the country. The memory of that day in December 1967, shortly before Christmas, remains clear in my mind. He had passed by to see us on his way back from Bethlehem, where he had spent the day. At that time there were no checkpoints, and we could travel all over historic Palestine without any problems. It seemed that while he was away from his house that day, the Israeli military forces had been searching for him and had cordoned off his family's house in Birzeit, as well as his sister's house in Ramallah. (This was the same sister with whom he had stayed in Nablus during Jordan's rule, and whose husband, the Reverend Elia Khoury, was eventually deported as well.) A friend called me at home to ask if Kamal was with us, because the Israeli military forces were looking for him and seemed determined to watch his home and his sister's home until he showed up. I begged him to stay in hiding in our neighborhood, but he completely refused to put anybody in harm's way, and decided to hand himself over as soon as he arrived in Ramallah. That was the last time I saw him. He spent that night in jail at the military occupation headquarters and was deported the next day, driving his own car across the bridge. (Even deportation had a honeymoon period. Later, people who were deported were simply thrown across the borders.) See Appendix I for the article that the Spectator wrote about Kamal's assassination.

Other family members suffered from Israeli occupation in other ways. My brother Hanna was in the States doing his graduate work at Purdue University when the country was occupied in 1967. He needed to apply for an Israeli visa on his Jordanian passport to enable him to return home. In the meantime, his wife applied for a family reunification permit for him, which helped in getting the visa. How ironic it was to have to go through this procedure simply in order to be back home with his family!

Hanna was again away on a sabbatical in 1971 when my father, who was president of the College, passed away, Hanna returned to carry on the legacy of Birzeit. Along with other college officials, mainly Dr. Gabi Baramki, he developed the college into a university. In 1973 Birzeit University became the first Palestinian University. However, Hanna's career was interrupted, and his life and that of his wife and four children was turned upside down overnight, when, on November 21, 1974, he was deported. This was a devastating experience for the whole family as well as for the university. Hanna had been called for a meeting at military headquarters in Ramallah on the evening of that day, but after that nobody seemed to know where he was. It was a day when all the population and the student body were out on the streets demonstrating in support of Yasser Arafat, chairman of the PLO, who had spoken at the United Nations for the first time. It was only the next day that we heard on the news that Hanna and four others had been deported and literally thrown across the Lebanese border.

The residents of Birzeit and Ramallah were not allowed to travel during that period, and a closure was imposed on the area due to the demonstrations in support of the PLO leader. However, there were no travel restrictions on residents of Jerusalem. As a result, I was the only one from the family who could travel via Jordan to Beirut to take Hanna some warm clothes and his Jordanian passport, since all his identification papers had been confiscated during deportation. From that day on, until he was eventually allowed to return home, I served as a liaison between Hanna and Birzeit University. In the meantime, Dr. Baramki, the academic vice president at the university, assumed the post of acting president. I stayed on as a volunteer for five years, working closely with Gabi and Ramzi Rihan, as well as with Fouad Ghawi on budgets and financial matters, as we prepared for the transition to a university. I helped in allocating housing for foreign teachers and recruiting office staff. While I was helping with human resources, I was ever so grateful for the support and wisdom of Hala Atallah, the student counselor, who was a great asset in solving personnel problems and conflicts. It was a great loss to the university and the community when she passed away after a very brief sickness in April 1995.

First graduation at Birzeit University, July 11, 1976

The first graduation in 1976 was a memorable occasion. This was the first graduating class of the first Palestinian university on Palestinian soil. I was heavily involved in the minutest details of that event, from ordering caps and gowns for the students and hoods for the teachers all the way to designing the diplomas and having them printed at the Commercial Press in Jerusalem. To give those graduates a special Palestinian look, Haifa Baramki helped design stoles with Palestinian embroidery, made at Inaash El Usrah, for each student to wear over his robe. I measured the head of each graduate and teacher at the time to confirm the correct sizes of the caps. We only received the caps half an hour before graduation. They had arrived at the airport the previous day, but the Israeli customs office would not release them. I could not have been more grateful to Kamal Shamhoum, our sports teacher, who set off that morning promising not to come back without those all-important graduation caps. And sure enough, he arrived just in time for everyone to snatch a cap irrespective of the list I had made. By the time everybody was in the procession I felt drained. Tears ran down my cheeks as the music for the procession started. Although Hanna was not with us physically, he was there in spirit as his voice came

Hanna welcomed back on campus with Dr. Baramki

Rima and Samia meeting Hanna at the border in Jericho

through the loudspeaker, delivering the graduation address that had been recorded abroad and smuggled into the country. There were yet more tears as everybody celebrated joyfully. For my husband and family it was a special celebration as I was spared a fatal accident the night before, when I fell asleep driving back home.

Hanna's deportation was such a brutal and unjust action that we were all so sure it would be a temporary measure. There were no charges, and the pressure from academic institutions, international organizations and churches seemed re-assuring. An Israeli physics professor, Daniel Amit, even offered to help fill in for Hanna's physics classes. Hanna himself went on speaking tours in the USA and Europe, emphasizing the illegality of deportation and his willingness to stand trial if need be. But like everything else since our dispossession, what seemed at the beginning to be a temporary measure ended up being a new permanent reality that we had to deal with. My mother passed away in 1986 without ever fulfilling her dream of seeing Hanna back home. When she needed surgery in 1985, we decided to take her to London so that Hanna could join us there. He, my sister and I rented a flat near the London Clinic where we spent time with our mother. When she finally had to return back home, we all realized it would be his last farewell to her.

I could write a saga about my trips to Amman and back. Ever since the Israeli occupation began, restrictions had been imposed on travel to Amman. One needed a special permit to cross on special buses. There were also restrictions as to what one could carry back from Jordan. All letters and printed material were censored. In addition, of course, Jordan imposed restrictions on Israeli products. Even the Israeli import tax label, which appeared in Hebrew on foreign products such as the Kolynos toothpaste, would be enough reason for the Jordanian officer to confiscate the product. What was important to them was not to see any Hebrew. And should we have a stamp on our passport to indicate that we had travelled via Lod airport, we would be in trouble for flying through an "enemy" airport.

YWCA Middle East Region at World Council, Stavangar, Norway

When, in 1994, peace was forged between Jordan and Israel and the relationship was normalized between the two countries, the change was sudden. Despite the ongoing occupation of the Palestinian Territories, overnight many things became permissible. However, despite the fact that the two countries are now at peace, the relationship continues to be quite unbalanced. For instance, Israelis can now drive in their cars to Jordan and have their visas stamped at the entrance port, whereas Jordanians still need a visa granted ahead of time by the Israeli Embassy in Jordan. This visa is not easily issued, and is very often denied altogether. This seems quite ironic in light of the "normal relationship" between the two countries.

The bus ride from Jericho across the Allenby Bridge to the Jordanian point of entry during those days was the prelude to a nightmare. I remember the bus, so crammed with passengers that it was like a can of sardines. One day, as we were waiting to head to Amman, the bus was so completely packed that there seemed not to be room for one more foot to step in. I asked the driver to get going, since the bus was full. He arrogantly responded that I should not expect him to move while there was yet room on the bus. With such logic, how could I respond? I simply had to shut up and wait. Nor were the taxis and the taxi drivers that picked us up from the arrival point in Jordan to Amman any better. One time, as I got into one of those dilapidated taxis, I jokingly told the Jordanian driver, "I bet there is a special catalog from which you order these cars." "What are you saying?" he inquired with annoyance. Lacking any sense of humor, he did not realize that I was commenting on the state of his taxi. And I am glad he did not, otherwise he might have thrown me out of the car!

If the ride to Jordan was the prelude, crossing back from Jordan to the Israeli side of the bridge was the real nightmare. The humiliation of the personal search, the stripping, the search for our own shoes amongst a stinking pile of travelers' footwear—a mélange of colors, sizes, and types, from sandals to slippers, tennis shoes, boots, flat shoes, high heels—left me numb at the end of the day. I felt haunted every time I needed to do that trip. It was our new Via Dolorosa. Occasionally we would even be asked about our faith, whether we were Christian or Muslim, which had nothing to do with security. Perhaps it was an attempt to drive a wedge amongst the Palestinians.

The most memorable experience I had at the bridge was one morning when some members of the Board of Trustees of Birzeit University and I were on our way to Amman to meet with Hanna, to discuss the by-laws of the university among other issues. As the Secretary of the Board at that time, I had a folder with all the necessary papers. At the time it was not at all the norm to search people as they were leaving the Israeli side of the bridge. However, the censor officer asked to have a look at my folder. I was waiting in line near Gabi Baramki, whose face and height were familiar to the Israeli Security due to the endless confrontations with Israeli forces at the university. A few days before our crossing, the Israeli army had invaded the men's dorms and pulled students out of their beds and showers.

A number of students were injured in that horrible and brutal confrontation. I remember taking more than five students to the hospital in Ramallah in my small Opel Kadet car. The Public Relations Office at the University issued a publication documenting the incident with photos, and I happened to be carrying three copies of those pamphlets along with other university papers.

My sister Rima was already waiting for me outside the hall when she saw the officer opening the folder. She immediately spotted the publications, and the stern look she gave me scared me more than the interrogation of the officer, who had already confiscated the whole folder. Of course, I could also read her lips as she mouthed hmarah (jack ass). On his next trip to Amman Gabi was asked whether he was carrying any papers, or whether he had had somebody carry them for him. For almost three years after that incident I was delayed and thoroughly searched on leaving and entering the country via the bridge. It was a real nightmare. One of the most humiliating experiences was when the security lady removed my sanitary napkin. I could not believe she would stoop to that level. In the process she said, "Sorry I have to do that." I answered that I was sorry for her. My letter to Mr. Shahal, the Minister of Police appears as Appendix II.

Fortunately, these memories are now behind me, especially now that the procedure of crossing has become slightly more civilized since the signing of the Oslo Accords. Besides, I do not need to cross as often as before. But I still remember that special day when my husband accompanied me to Amman. The bridge was crowded and one elderly man wearing the traditional head dress (hatta and Iqal) was pushing his way through to get to the bus. In fact I think everybody was trying to push their way through, but it seemed that this foreign tourist, who was wearing a hat was getting nervous and took it up on the man with the head dress. At that time there wasn't a special lane for foreigners. He just picked up his head dress and shouted at him to get back in line. As the poor man scurried to find his hatta and Iqal my husband picked up the tourist's hat and flipped it away as far as he could. "Why did you do that?" the shocked tourist shouted. "Because you humiliated that man" my husband responded, and continued to explain to the tourist that in our culture this is considered an insult. Well that tourist must have had the lesson of his life time.

My trips to Amman began long before Hanna was deported, since I was regularly on the road for YWCA (Young Women's Christian Association) meetings. When the YWCA of Palestine ceased to exist after 1948, some of its members who ended up in Amman and East Jerusalem, along with others from Jordan, reestablished the YWCA in Amman, East Jerusalem and Jericho. Together, these branches formed the National YWCA of Jordan, with the national office in Jerusalem. Later on, two more associations were established in Madaba and El-Husson. In 1967, the YWCA in the Occupied Territories remained part of the Jordan National YWCA. It was only after King Hussein disengaged from the Palestinian Territories in 1988 that the situation changed. By mutual agreement with the YWCA of Jordan it was decided to reestablish the national association of Palestine as an independent body. Its affiliation to the World YWCA movement was approved with flying flags at the World Council meeting in Stavanger, Norway in 1991. I was privileged to be the first National President of the YWCA of Palestine. To date, the Palestine YWCA has associations in Jerusalem, Ramallah and Jericho. While serving two terms as national president of the YWCA of Jordan, I frequently travelled that path of humiliation across the bridge with Doris Salah, the General Secretary. During security checks I often heard Doris arguing with the female security guard in the cubicle next to mine. When the guard ordered, "Ishlakh, take off your clothes," Doris challenged the guard to use the metal detector instead. "Why do they give you these machines?" she asked. "Aren't you supposed to use them?"

Despite all the humiliation, you cannot but notice the humorous side of things. There were so many funny episodes. I especially remember the way they called our Arabic names on the Israeli side,

Samia with Mrs. Awad and Mrs. Sukkar – YWCA of Jordan

and our foreign names, such as Doris, Joyce, Jean or Claudette on the Jordanian side. I suppose pronouncing foreign names is always problematic to locals, wherever they are. But on the bridge such episodes provided badly needed comic relief from the indignities we suffered. Up to this day, we often spend evenings reminiscing over those experiences, trying to forget all the bitterness and simply remember the good days with our colleagues in Jordan. I still carry lovely memories and deep appreciation for those dedicated and committed women leaders and founders who had such an impact on my involvement in the YWCA, especially Mrs. Sukkar, Mrs. Shuweihat and Mrs. Awad.

One time, as I was in line on the Jordanian side, I heard the officer tell a wretched old woman ahead of me that she would not be allowed to cross to Jordan unless she had the exact address of where she was planning to stay. It was quite an absurd request: there were few street names at that time in Jordan, and what street names existed were mostly in Amman, the capital city. It took almost an essay for her to describe where she was going, probably a far away place. When my turn came I felt so proud of myself that I actually knew the exact address of my cousin Fouad Farradj. With his dry expression, perhaps thinking that we didn't deserve any better, the officer sternly asked about my address. I said Ba'ounieh Street, Jabal Lewibdeh, near the Lewibdeh mosque. I thought I had gotten it right, and what better landmark than the famous mosque? He looked me straight in the face and asked, "What is the closest zubermarket (Supermarket)?" I did not dare laugh: I knew for a fact that if the border personnel lacked anything, it was a sense of humor. On another occasion I was saved by Subhi Khoury, whom I did not know personally at the time. He had a pharmaceutical company in Birzeit, and heard me arguing with the Jordanian officer, who was insisting on confiscating the Birzeit university catalogs because printed material from Israel was banned, and I was insisting that Birzeit was not in Israel.

It was quite a relief when my official trips to Amman came to an end. There were no YWCA meetings any more, and my brother Hanna was eventually allowed to come back home. His return on April 30, 1993, along with that of twenty others, was considered at the time a good-will gesture on the part of Israel to prove that it was serious about the peace process.

The peace process had started with the Madrid Conference at the end of October 1991, and was followed by the Oslo Accords, which were eventually signed in September 1993. My sister and I were amongst thousands of people—families, friends and scouts—waiting for hours near the border in Jericho to welcome the returnees back. The joy of seeing Hanna kissing the ground as he and his wife stepped off that homecoming bus brought tears of joy to our eyes. It was an overwhelming experience that no words could express. As we drove past Abu-Qash, the little village before Birzeit, his dream of seeing the new campus with the buildings that he had helped raise funds for was finally realized. The first place he visited in Birzeit was the graveyard, where he laid flowers on mother's tombstone. Two days later, on Sunday, we celebrated with a thanksgiving service at the church. The welcome he had on campus after the weekend was memorable. It was too bad that mother was not there to share this momentous occasion with us. She never gave up hope that he would return one day. Fortunately, Aunt Aniseh, our only surviving aunt among my father's eight sisters, had kept on holding the fort. Aunt Aniseh passed away a few years after Hanna's return. As I look back at those long years of futile peace negotiations and the deadlock in the peace process, I sometimes feel that maybe the only positive thing that came out of the signing of the Oslo Accords was that Hanna, and so many other Palestinians, were able to return home.

Occupation is indeed brutal, and spares none. In fact, there wasn't one family that did not have its share of suffering during those years of the *Intifada*. In 1988, our son Suhail spent six months in jail for producing a tape of popular folk songs with alternative lyrics that glorified the *Intifada*. July 4, 1988 began as a normal day. Suhail walked into the kitchen to ask me if he could borrow my car for a few hours, as it was more dependable than his car. He was making a trip to Tel Aviv to pick up some tapes. My car, an Opel Ascona, was practically new at the time. At around four in the afternoon, a young boy showed up at our doorstep asking for Suhail, who was supposed to give him a music lesson. Yousef was very upset with Suhail for making an appointment and not keeping it. We failed to realize then and there that he had been "kidnapped." But when he did not show up by ten in the evening, we knew there was something very wrong. We contacted a lawyer, who confirmed our suspicions. Suhail and the car were being held at the police station in Jerusalem, known as the "Maskoubieh"—the Russian compound. When we were allowed to visit him, after 24 hours, the police guard would not permit me to get close to him. I insisted that as a mother I had the right to hug him. He finally allowed me to do so, provided we didn't speak a word to each other. I did manage an "Allah Ma'ak" (God be with you) after seeing how bruised his neck was, presumably from torture. When they brought him to the court room the next day, he pointed at the hand cuffs and shackles on his feet and said to me: "Tell your American friends these are made in the USA."

During my visits to jail I built a comradeship with other mothers, sisters and wives of prisoners that lasted long after our young men were released. The other women even gave me tips on how to smuggle in a few mint leaves, a small treat that Suhail loved with his tea. Did the Israelis really think a few leaves of mint would threaten the security of the prison? I remember that on one of my visits the prison authorities did not allow me to bring Suhail some warm flannel shirts; I was asked to leave them at the desk outside the visiting area. The shirts eventually disappeared; Suhail never received them, nor were they found so I could take them back home. Similarly, the tapes he had made were confiscated, yet we had to pay the studio for them. My car, which Suhail had used to pick up the tapes, was confiscated as well, because according to the military court it was the "vehicle that carried the inciting material." "What if he had used the Egged bus (Israeli public transportation) to carry the tapes?" I asked the Attorney General. But I never got an answer. So when they announced Suhail's jail sentence—18 months imprisonment, with twelve months suspended—I simply looked at the Attorney General and said, "Enjoy the tape." I must admit he was very cordial to me. Had we met under different circumstances, we might have found a lot to discuss. However, his persistence on replaying in the courtroom the section of the tape that said, "the voice of the *Intifada* is higher than the voice of the occupation," must have affected the decision of the Judge. Meanwhile, my car received a life sentence and was never released, not even after Suhail had served his term. I do not know if the expression of life sentence is applicable to vehicles, but under military occupation, anything is applicable, and the factory of words can produce any terminology. Ironically, however, while Suhail was serving his sentence, the tape was being sold in the local market. We always wondered who the supplier was, since the tapes had all been confiscated.

As I sat at home reflecting on the absurdity of this incident, my memories carried me back to three years earlier when Suhail came home carrying a large poster. As he unrolled it to hang in his room, I watched with interest to see who he was the latest fan of. No, it was not rock star Elton John or Bruce Springsteen. Nor was it any of his childhood favorites, Curious George or Snoopy. As I watched, I realized that my son was no longer a child. All of a sudden he was grown up, an adult. The poster was a picture of a soldier kneeling in front of a row of helmets and guns. Above the soldier was a large heading: WHY? Looking at it, I realized that there was too much suffering and injustice around Suhail. His eyes expressed the struggle going on in his mind. Why did young soldiers have to die, and for what? Why do people have to go on suffering because of so much greed, injustice and oppression? Is not peace an alternative? Will we ever see a world void of armament and wars? Will we ever enjoy peace in our lifetimes? At what price?

The day Suhail was to be released was Thursday, December 22, 1988. I had contacted the lawyer twice before that day to be sure everything was proceeding according to schedule. After the long drive of almost three hours to Atlit prison, which is near Haifa in northern Israel, we were told his release would be the next day. I almost flipped out at the reason they gave for the delay. Indeed, it was quite a paradox. Because the prison authorities thought he was Muslim, they had intended to release him on Thursday to be with his family on Friday, the Muslim holiday. But since they had just found out that he was Christian, he would now be released on Friday so as to be with his family on Sunday, the Christian holiday. (Saturday is the Jewish holiday, and they do not release anybody on that day.) How kind of them to take his religious holiday into consideration after he had missed so many Sundays already! What difference would one day have made for the jail authority is beyond me. At that moment I actually wished I were an atheist so that nobody could abuse our faith in such a ridiculous manner. If the Israeli intelligence officers were really so smart they would have known that Khoury is a Christian family name. But the reason they gave was not valid in any case. Suhail's term would have ended after Christmas, but because his release was close to Christmas time the judge took that into consideration and set the day for his release a few days before Christmas. So the whole episode was simply a further harassment from the prison authorities, not for Suhail only, but for us as a family.

I must admit that the guard at the gate outside, who was a Druze soldier, felt for me and was quite compassionate. Khalto (aunty) he said: "Please go and come back tomorrow." I eventually realized it would be futile to just hang around frustrated. We had no mobiles at the time, so I could not call the lawyer or the family. We did not, however, come back empty handed. We found a young man at the gate who had been released without prior notice. There he was, standing at the gate looking completely lost, as there was nobody there to pick him up. So we took him with us. The prison authorities released those who did not expect to be released, and held those who did. It reminded me of our confession prayer: "We did things that we should not do and left undone things that we should do." Well, at least one family on the Mt. of Olives was happily surprised, even though everybody at our home was disappointed. My sister Rima, the composer in the family, who was still able to come to Jerusalem at that time, was there with a welcoming song for him. My sisters-in-law had also helped in preparing the traditional date cookies to offer to guests who would come to congratulate us upon Suhail's release. But Rima's song had to wait for the next day, and I completely lost my appetite for the delicious food she had prepared for the family reunion lunch.

Those years of the *Intifada* brought so much suffering upon so many families. But the spirit of solidarity and struggle united us as one community. Our efforts to plan and carry out innovative and resourceful ideas to challenge the harsh measures of the occupation kept us going, full of hope and determination. For instance, during the *Intifada*, leaflets with directives for a whole week would be left on the streets of each neighborhood. Almost everybody abided by

The release of Suhail from jail with his cousin Nadim Tony and friend Abu Ata

the instructions for strikes, protests and days of fasting. We were also urged to have our own vegetable gardens and to plant every empty plot so as to supply ourselves and our neighbors with vegetables, as these were completely unavailable in the market due to the prolonged curfews. To make up for the closure of schools, alternative classrooms ran in private homes in every neighborhood. Bread and milk were left for families at their doorsteps during curfews. The spirit of solidarity was amazing, and it worried the Israeli Occupation Forces. I recall the case of a young boy at the Qalandia refugee camp who was picked up by the Israeli soldiers. Immediately, around ten women barged in to save him, each claiming he was her son. The soldier was dumbfounded. He exclaimed he had heard of ten fathers claiming the same son, but ten mothers was something new!!

The refugee camps where the YWCA had centers were exposed to particular harassment, especially the Jalazoun Camp. During curfews, some of those phenomenal women from the camps would find a way to get to the YWCA in Jerusalem to seek help and to obtain food supplies. Doris Salah, General Secretary at that time, went out of her way to support those women. Whenever she had guests she would take them to visit Jalazoun, Qalandia and Aqabet Jaber. The YWCA of Jerusalem became a centre of leadership training as well as a comforting haven for women and young people of different ages and social backgrounds, away from the restrictions and the depressive life under occupation. Aside from the regular summer camps, it provided cultural programs such as art, music and folk dancing, as well as political debates and panels. It was heavily involved in advocating and monitoring human rights, long before any national organizations were established for that purpose. With the help of a good team of speakers from the members of the YWCA, and from the community as well, Doris never missed an opportunity to educate church groups and others about our Palestinian cause and struggle for liberation. The YWCA at the time had a hotel, so it was a good venue for those groups seeking the truth. Very often the YWCA in Jerusalem hosted women from the three refugee camps, offering special programs and a lunch, while inviting teenagers to join the summer camps for youth held in Ramallah. These were very meaningful encounters for everyone involved, including the Jerusalem YWCA women.

Since the closure of Jerusalem the women from the camps have not had access to the YWCA of Jerusalem. The loss is on both sides, for those women from the camps had many stories to tell. Even after the peace process, things did not change much for them. They were not spared the raids of settlers. Some of them lost hope. Others became very bitter and angry, while others were determined to stay put and make the best out of a bad situation. I remember that during one of those lunches that were possible in better times, we had asked those women to express their hopes for the future. Sadly, one of the women expressed the wish that her son would never grow up, so that he would not be harassed by the Israeli forces and spend his youth in Israeli jails.

The Heart-Broken Child

Looking back, I do not think I felt as distressed when my son Suhail was not released from prison as promised on December 22, 1988 as I was when I heard my heart-broken grandson, two years old at the time, telling me how naughty the police were at the airport because they did not allow his father into the country.

It was the morning of May 4, 1990, a lovely spring day that had started with joy, hope and laughter. My husband had accompanied my daughter, Dina, and her little boy Omar, to the airport to meet her husband, Yousef Nasser (who happens to have the same first name as my husband). Yousef was arriving from England where he had been working on his PhD.

For the previous week Omar had been talking about Baba (daddy) coming home. He was fully awake by 4:00 a.m. and ready for the drive to the airport. I stayed behind to prepare breakfast. But Omar's father never showed up. Although he was on the BA flight arriving from London at 4:45 a.m., he was refused entry to the country. The reason given was that he had overstayed the time allowed by his visa the last time he was in the country. Security put him back on the same plane, which took off at 8:15 that same morning, without allowing him to inform his family or even deliver the few gifts and goodies he had brought with him.

Our daughter Dina and her family in 1995

The real drama started when one of the passengers, who was on the same plane as Yousef, told Dina that Yousef was having a problem. Dina called me to let me know, in case I could reach the US embassy or a lawyer. Unfortunately, I did not succeed in reaching anybody at that unearthly hour. In the meantime, Dina barged into the arrival area, with Omar sitting in one of the luggage trolleys, and started calling out for Yousef. But he was nowhere to be found. She was picked up by the police for being in a restricted area, and falsely charged with assaulting the police as she pushed her way in. Of course she denied that strongly, and tried to explain the human aspect of the whole episode, but to no avail. She was taken with Omar in the van to the police station for the necessary formalities and fingerprints, after which her father had to bail her out. What an experience it must have been for a two-year-old child. All he could say, when they came back empty handed, with tears in his eyes, was, "naughty police."

I did not have a computer or access to e-mail at that time. But I was so distressed when I heard the story that I sat down immediately and typed out a letter to all the friends and human rights organizations I knew, circulating it by fax. I think that eventually the pressure helped; finally the lawyer was able to get him back in. In fact, it was another lawyer who had advised Yousef to stay longer when his initial visa expired, because he was trying to help get the request of our daughter for family reunification approved. Yousef had no residency permit in the country, because he was an American citizen. Eventually he managed to obtain the right of family reunification through his elderly aunt, who was living alone in Birzeit, not through his wife, who was living in Jerusalem. Little did we know at the time that the West Bank residency was going to be another nightmare for this young couple, since the whole area was under military occupation.

At the time, the young couple were living in the basement flat of our house in Jerusalem, and their three children were born in Jerusalem. Yousef used to commute easily to Birzeit, where he was teaching economics at Birzeit University. In fact, residents of both the West Bank and Jerusalem could at that time travel freely to all parts of historic Palestine that had become Israel in 1948. Ironically, it was only after the signing of the Oslo Peace Accords in 1993 that East Jerusalem ceased to be accessible to Palestinian residents from the West Bank. The only exceptions were for those with special permits, which were given only for a reason that the occupation authorities considered valid, such as a medical check up, or for special religious holidays. I remember at the time a friend telling me that she had overheard an elderly woman at the checkpoint pleading with the soldier to let her in. When he asked her if she had a permit, she simply told him that her eyes were yearning to see the city of Jerusalem. Even people who have lived all their lives in Jerusalem are now yearning to see the city. They have been deprived of this simple right under various pretexts, mostly racist ones, because Israel wants a minimum number of Palestinians in the city. Moreover, Palestinians who carry foreign passports and are living abroad, but who still maintain their West Bank identity cards, are not allowed to enter Jerusalem when they come to visit the country.

Marrying somebody from outside Jerusalem can be reason enough to justify one of the devious measures that cost Palestinians the right of residency in Jerusalem. A mixed marriage normally refers to a marriage between two people from two different faiths. At one time even a marriage between Catholics and non-Catholic Christians was considered a mixed marriage. But like everything else in our part of the world, and especially under a military occupation, familiar terminology—in this case, "mixed marriage"—can mean something else completely. Language becomes a tool to twist and use to suit the purposes and policies of the occupation authorities.

In a letter to the BBC dated August 9, 2001, Dr. Hanan Ashrawi objected to the use of the term "targeted killings," the latest Israeli-British euphemism for extra-judicial assassinations. It seems now that the occupiers and their allies are adding yet more distortions to their long list of contradictory terminology. The Israeli Military Forces are called the Israeli *Defense Forces*. The Palestinian dispossession (the *Nakba*) is called by the Israelis the 1948 *War of Independence*. The 1967 offensive became a war of *liberation*, while resisting the occupation is called *terrorism*. The list goes on and on. But what remains on top of the list is the usage of the term "security measures" for violations of human rights. The justification of any action as a security measure prohibits questioning those measures or holding Israel accountable to international law. Even the Occupied Territories, which are recognized by both international law and the United Nations as Occupied Territories, have been sugar coated with a variety of definitions: first, they were known as the "liberated territories," then they were termed "administered territories," and last but not least, they have become "disputed territories." We should not be surprised, therefore, that the BBC succumbed to the pressure of using the term "targeted killings" instead of "assassinations." After all, euphemism is an English word and was probably created to deal with the way the British would have liked to portray matters. Language is a reflection of how people think, but it also shapes the narrative.

I still remember an experience that my father shared with us in 1946, shortly before he resigned as one of the assistants to the General Secretary of the British Mandate in Jerusalem, due to the British policy regarding Jewish immigration. The General Secretary showed him a letter he was planning to send, and asked what my father thought of it. My father read it more than once, and commented that it was not clear, and that he could not understand what was meant by the text. "That is exactly the idea," responded the General Secretary. It is not surprising that the UN Security Council Resolution 242, passed after the 1967 war, which was sponsored by the British ambassador Lord Caradon, was just as vague. Notably, it stipulated the withdrawal of Israel from "territories" occupied in the recent conflict, not "The Territories." This small matter of language was to become part of Israel's rational for why it should not return the Occupied Territories to Palestinians.

With all this twisted terminology, it is no surprise that a mixed marriage for Palestinians in Jerusalem has nothing to do with one's faith or church affiliation. When a Jerusalem resident finds a spouse from outside the Jerusalem area, or, now, from behind the "Separation Wall"[1], who has no "right" of residency in the city, this is called a "mixed marriage." In fact, such an arrangement is much more complicated than a mixed marriage between a Christian and a Muslim or a Jew. Nowadays many people think twice before they start dating someone from outside their area.

At a wedding at the Church of the Augusta Victoria on the Mt. of Olives, at which the Lutheran Bishop was officiating, the wedding

---

1 A concrete wall that Israel started building in 2002 to separate the Palestinian territories from Israel. 85% of the wall is built on Palestinian land. The wall separates Palestinians from Palestinians as well as from their land and their community services.

entourage was late because the bride lived behind the checkpoint. My brother-in-law suggested to the Bishop that it would be very appropriate to include, along with the traditional vows, "for richer for poorer, in sickness and in health," a contemporary vow, "within checkpoints or outside checkpoints."

The ordeals that two young women from Jerusalem, Mona Nasir Tucktuck and Zeina Ashrawi Hutchison, faced during their last visits to Jerusalem with their families in the summer of 2008, in incidents that received wide publicity at that time, are examples of how a normal love affair leading to marriage can become a nightmare to a Jerusalemite whose spouse is from outside Jerusalem. Both Mona and Zeina married Palestinian American citizens, and are living in the United States. When they came to visit during the summer holidays, they discovered that the Israeli authorities had cancelled their right of residency[2] in Jerusalem, and that they had a limited time to stay in the country. Israel has annexed Jerusalem, and considers it the "eternal capital of Israel," but it continues to apply absurd laws to the non-Jewish residents of the city. Israelis can live as long as they wish outside the country, and can carry more than one passport, while at the same time maintaining their right of residency once they decide to come back to the country. In contrast, the safest guarantee for young Palestinians in Jerusalem is to find their sweethearts from their own neighborhoods, so as not to lose their basic right to reside in their home town. The bride can walk out of her house into the house of her neighbor, as it is described in the famous Arabic folk song, "tala'ah min beit abouha, dakhleh beit el jeeran." But so often Cupid's arrow goes beyond walls and checkpoints, and young couples continue to pay the price.

Hundreds of Palestinians have been deprived of their right of residency in Jerusalem simply because they have been out of the country for more than seven years. This especially affects students,

---

2 Although Israel annexed Jerusalem, Palestinian Jerusalemites are granted a residency permit in the form of an Identity Card. This ID card needs to be renewed, and can be revoked for a number of reasons.

even when they return home every summer. My husband's nephew, Ramzi Baramki, is one of those whose residency card or Identity Card has been revoked. Ironically, Prime Minister Netanyahu himself spent more than seven years outside Israel. It is only in Israel that birthright residency can be withdrawn at the whim and wish of the Ministry of Interior, simply because one is not a Jew. When a spouse is from outside Jerusalem, it takes a scratch of a pen to cancel the Jerusalem Identity Card (ID) of the other spouse. In contrast, for the spouse to reunite with the spouse that has a Jerusalem ID requires a very long procedure, and often becomes mission impossible. My own daughter had to seek the services of a lawyer in order to retrieve her Jerusalem Identity Card when the Israeli Ministry of Interior cancelled it because her husband had a West Bank Identity Card. She was unable to register her youngest son, Faris, at the Ministry of Interior for a birth certificate until he was six years old. Unfortunately, the nightmare is not over. Their residency is continuously challenged, since approval for family reunification with her husband has not yet been granted. When President Clinton visited Jerusalem in 1998, my husband and I wrote the following letter to him about the matter. Although we included our address and phone number, we never received a response. A copy of the letter appears as Appendix III.

Closure of the Alley

We woke up one morning to the sounds of digging on our street. Rushing out to see what was happening, we found that the military had given instructions to close the road that led to the main entrance of our house. As usual, we were informed that the closure was necessary for "security reasons," a gimmick Israel has long used to get away with all its illegal actions and violations of the rights of Palestinians.

In this case, the "security issue" at stake was the need to protect the Israeli Military Central Command headquarters. As if the military occupation itself was not enough, shortly after 1967 the Israelis had built their military headquarters on top of the mountain directly behind our house, using confiscated Palestinian land for the purpose. We had a heated argument with the military, and eventually succeeded in convincing them to move the closure further away from the entrance of our house. Barbed wire was put up at the end of the alley, and our house marked a dead end. That meant that there was no longer access leading to the rest of the neighborhood. Eventually the municipality had to open another road for the residents in our area.

I was so furious at the closure that when one of the workers, who unfortunately was Palestinian, asked for a drink of water, I snapped at him and told him to go and get a drink from his masters who were paying him to do the job. After I walked into the house, I could not believe that this was me who was refusing a drink of water to anybody! Still shaking with anger about the whole incident, I opened the door to a visitor, my Aunt Victoria, who was a social worker living in Nablus. "Is it true you refused a drink of water to the worker?" she asked. The man had apparently asked her to intervene.

"What happened to you?" she began. "What happened to all the values that you were brought up with as a human being? What about our Palestinian hospitality?" she continued prodding.

"All gone," I snapped back. "I am so angry at the military occupation that I took it out on this poor laborer." We both looked at each other and started laughing as I went to fetch that glass of water. I knew, then and there, that I should not let the occupation get to me if I wanted to maintain my sanity and humanity without hatred and bitterness.

My brother Hanna had a similar experience when he refused a drink of water to a soldier who came knocking at our door in Birzeit. My father came to the rescue and rebuked my brother. "Do you think you are going to solve the Palestinian issue with a glass of water?" Once again, it was the same aunt, Victoria, who told us that she had given a lift to an Israeli soldier on her way from Nablus to a family gathering in Birzeit. My sister and I could not believe our ears. We attacked her like vultures. "How could you?" we demanded. "They are the occupiers!" But with her usual hearty laugh she justified her action. "It was a very hot day, and I felt sorry for the soldier, who looked so young." All we could do was join in her laughter and enjoy some humor, which always helped us cope.

At the end of the day I was not terribly upset about the dead end, for it eventually stopped the soldiers from passing in front of our house to get to the Central Command. Very often they were a nuisance, as they provoked our dogs to start barking at them. One day my husband caught a soldier spitting and throwing a stone at one of the dogs. When he shouted at him and rebuked him for doing so, the soldier claimed that the dog scared him. My husband told him that it was really ridiculous for a soldier in an army that stood against all the Arab countries to be scared by a dog behind a gate. Eventually we found both dogs dead. It was such a stormy and rainy day that as we dragged the drenched corpses to their burial at the edge of the garden we could not determine whether they had been shot or poisoned. We were almost sure it was the work of some of those soldiers, since nobody else used the alley. It also must have been one of the soldier's cigarette stubs that triggered a fire one evening in the bushes close to our gate.

On the other hand, one day when I was trying to open the gate while carrying some bags, a soldier passing by stopped to help me. It was so difficult for me to say thank you at the time that I simply forced a smile and a nod. Once again I forgot all about my humanity. In a split second I envisaged this extended hand as the hand that could have shot my cousin or thrown my brother in the jeep to be deported, or maybe the hand that had hand-cuffed my son to take him to jail.

Shortly after that incident, we were having a meeting of the organization Sabeel. The group was in its founding stages, and we had not yet chosen a name for this Palestinian Liberation Theology movement. I felt good to be able to share that incident and that of the glass of water with the group, and to talk about forgiveness and reconciliation. What a difference between my reaction then and my response the day that Josef Ben Eliezer spoke in Nazareth at the Sabeel 7th international conference.

Physically a short small man, Josef Ben Eliezar stood tall as he asked for forgiveness from the Palestinians. The occasion was the conference on "The *Nakba*: Memory, Reality and Beyond," which took place in Nazareth and Jerusalem in November 2008. Eliezar shared with the participants his testimony of being an Israeli soldier in 1948. He described taking part in the expulsion of the Palestinian population from Lydda and robbing them of their money and

Samia with Josef Ben Eliezer at the Sabeel Conference in Nazareth

personal possessions. Josef could not live with the reality of that day in July 1948. He realized that what he had done to the Palestinians was what the Nazis had done to his people and to his family before he emmigrated from Germany to Palestine after the Holocaust. He did not find a listening ear in the newly established state of Israel. The inhumanity of that war, which as a Jew he had believed was a war of liberation and independence, haunted him until he eventually left the country and settled in England.

I wonder how many Israelis would have the courage and the magnanimity of Josef to admit that they have done the Palestinians wrong, let alone to ask for forgiveness. Although his testimony was mostly in front of an international audience, there were a number of Palestinians from Jerusalem and Nazareth who heard him loud and clear. I was so moved that I stood up and recognized his courage, thanking him for his testimony and assuring him that we do forgive him. I thought of the Bible passage in which Peter asks, "Lord, how many times shall I forgive my brother when he sins against me? Up to seven times?" Jesus answered, "I tell you, not seven times, but seventy times seven times" (Matthew 18:21-22).

As people came up to thank me later for my words, I could not help but wonder how meaningful it would have been for the Palestinian people, and how much suffering could have been spared, had the Israelis, since day one of the establishment of the state in 1948, admitted the grave injustice they had inflicted upon the Palestinians, asked for forgiveness, and allowed all who were evicted to return to their homes. This is a dream that could still be realized if the Jewish people would ponder and act in accordance with the words of their great prophet Micah: "What does the Lord require of you but to do justice, to love kindness, and to walk humbly with your God" (Micah 6:8).

As the situation continued to deteriorate, it was not surprising that we blamed the occupation for everything that went wrong. Our lives had been turned upside down ever since Israel succeeded in taking over our country on that fateful day of June 5, 1967. I remember how, in the early days after 1967, we did not worry much about finding the right school for the children because they were still young and they were going to the nursery school of the Rosary Sisters very close to our house. We were sure that by the time they were ready for school this whole nightmare would be over. Now that they are parents themselves, and some of the grandchildren are already in college, I realize how over-optimistic we were. As the years went by, the new reality on the ground has become so entrenched that it ceased to be a temporary measure anymore. In fact, it continues to affect every aspect of our lives. With every step we take, wherever we are heading, there is always a big surprise, a new road, a new checkpoint, or a new geography and a new reality to deal with.

For my mother, this new reality brought back memories of the curse of misfortune, "May your chest be locked" (Yeqfil sidrek), which she had heard the women of Nablus use when we lived there in the early forties. It was only after the occupation that she was able to comprehend the real meaning of such a curse, and what it implied. Not only were our chests locked, but so were our dreams, our hopes, our plans and our whole future.

That is exactly the feeling that settled over me when I saw the Separation Wall for the first time. I felt my chest lock. It hit me right in the face. And now this infamous wall, which Israel considers a "security fence," has become another reality on the ground. For the Mennonite Central Committee (MCC) July-September 2004 newsletter I contributed the following article on the Wall:

"Good fences make good neighbors" is an English saying. But this so-called "security fence" is neither good nor is it a fence. It is an evil barrier that will exacerbate the dehumanization of a whole population. Israel uses the word "security" because it has very skillfully put its security as a priority on the agenda of the world conscience. Israel thus avoids being challenged.

Humans erect psychological barriers between themselves based on looks, religion, race, or social class. The separation wall might be the first physical barrier that Israel is erecting, but in reality the process of putting up legal and psychological walls started with the establishment of the state of Israel in 1948, and continued with the occupation of the Palestinian territories in 1967.

The decision for the state to be a Jewish state, rather than a state of all of its citizens, was in itself a decision to establish a wall between the Jews of the new state and the non-Jewish population, the indigenous Palestinians. Those Palestinians who were dispossessed of their land and identity by the creation of the state of Israel found themselves to be either stateless refugees or second-class citizens of the new Jewish state. Through "legal" legislation many more walls were erected within the state of Israel—laws that restricted Palestinian access to land, that limited the possibilities of developing Palestinian cities and towns—turning it gradually into an apartheid state with different sets of laws for Jews and Arabs.

Using biblical texts to justify confiscation of more land after its military occupation of the West Bank, East Jerusalem, and the Gaza Strip in 1967, a confiscation that paved the way for building exclusively Jewish settlements, spelled another chapter in the building of walls and barriers. The Separation Wall now being built is but the latest and most obvious of Israel's discriminatory walls.

It is amazing how the international community can stand helpless against the new reality of the Separation Wall. Though European countries were critical of Israel for constructing the Separation Wall, they abstained when the United Nations voted to take the case to the International Court of Justice at The Hague. How hypocritical! The U.N. resolution passed, but its impact was watered down by the abstentions and by the usual U.S. vote against any resolution condemning Israel.

I cannot help but recall the words of Edmund Burke: "The only thing necessary for the triumph of evil is for good people to do nothing." That is exactly what the story of our dispossession as a people, as well as the story of this Wall, has been about. Good and responsible people can understand the discriminatory realities, but are often afraid to expose the truth for fear of being labeled anti-Semitic. The truth of the Wall has nothing to do with anti-Semitism, and it is the duty of good people not to allow the triumph of evil. "You shall know the truth, and the truth shall set you free" (John 8:32).

Will the world community continue to be intimidated? Some refuse: think of the many activists, Israelis and Palestinians, as well as members of the international solidarity movement, who, with their relentless efforts, have been able to expose the truth regarding the Separation Wall. They have been putting themselves in places of danger to emphasize the gravity of building such a wall and its impact on the soul of the people on both sides of the wall.

Israel claims to want this "security fence" in order to separate the Palestinians from the Israelis, and to prevent the infiltration of Palestinians into Israel. This justification might have been acceptable had the wall been erected on the 1967 border, with a full withdrawal

My parents, Musa and Linda Nasir

from the occupied territories in accordance with UN Security Council Resolutions 242 and 338. But as it is now, and with Israel defying all UN resolutions, the wall is actually separating Palestinians from Palestinians. It is also separating Palestinians from their land, work, hospitals, schools, churches, and mosques, and from their families and the center of their lives. The wall, in brief, makes normal life practically impossible for the Palestinians.

I sincerely hope that Israel will realize that to guarantee its security, it has to see the other as a human being. It was the inclusive theology of Jesus and the face-to-face encounter with the Samaritan woman at Jacob's well that pulled down the walls between Jew and Samaritan when Jesus asked for a drink of water (John 4:1-42).

Both my parents died after the occupation began, without realizing their dream of restoring justice and living in peace in a pluralistic secular Palestine. Yet in spite of all that has happened, and the hopelessness of the situation, my father never relinquished his efforts in pursuit of a just solution, though he realized it was a long struggle. He used to tell me that I would be very fortunate if my grandchildren would see a solution to the conflict. He felt strongly about the Golden Rule[3], which he thought would be an ideal motto for humanity and would solve so many problems, since there is reference to it in practically all faiths. That is why he was disappointed with the churches for being influenced by theological interpretations as well as vested interests of politicians. He was almost sure that had the churches raised their voice loud enough in 1948 against that grave injustice, it might have been possible then and there to redress that injustice at an earlier stage, and even help in the return of the Palestinian refugees. In hindsight, we cannot absolve some of the Arab countries, although we realize how weak and manipulated they were at the time (and although they continue to be manipulated up to this day).

My mother never lost her faith, and was continuously grateful to God for many blessings, despite all the brutality that we had to face on a daily basis. Very often I used to tease her and urge her to challenge the good Lord and demand some justice. On her deathbed in January 1986, we would hear her thanking God, but there would always be a mutter at the end: "If only...if only..." We understood that the only thing she was yearning for was to see my brother Hanna, her only son, who was still living in exile. But that is the sad story of so many Palestinian mothers who died while waiting for the return of their children or for their release from Israeli jails.

After watching my mother losing her battle with cancer, my sister Rima and I felt like it was the end of an era for us. Although my father had passed away fifteen years earlier, we still felt that home was home, as his spirit and possessions were still there where my mother was. But now they were both gone, and it felt like the place had lost its soul. The loss was very painful. My parents were very

---

3 The Golden Rule appears in more than one Gospel: "Do to others what you would have them do to you" (Matthew 7:12). The same concept is referred to in Islam (Hadith,) Judaism (Talmud), Buddhism (Udana-Varga), Hinduism (The Mahabharata), Zoroastrianism (Shayast-na-Shayast 13:29), and Baha'I (Epistle to the Son of the Wolf, 30).

Rev. Naim Ateek with the executive of Sabeel Jean, Samia, and Cedar and staff member Nora

special. Although we had spent our school days as boarders, the time we had with them during weekends and holidays was quality time. My father was so humble; his main concern was always the public welfare. The word "I" was taboo in the family vocabulary. He never boasted about his achievements, nor did he allow us to do so. What was important to him always was that the work was done, and whatever we set out to achieve was accomplished. My mother was so compassionate, and her resilience and her loving care for others has always been an inspiration for us as a family and for all those whose lives she touched. She was the grand lady of the house, the hostess and mother image for the students. All the moral values that we adhere to are due to the way our parents brought us up. I was specially privileged to have worked with my father, not only in administration but also as his private secretary, where I learned so many life skills that no university could have ever taught me.

Very often I used to accompany my father to the YMCA when my uncle Labib Nasir, the general secretary, would invite him to speak to groups about the political situation. Many years later after the establishment of Sabeel, one of the main programs we had was to speak to groups. I could not help but think how Rev. Ateek, the founder and director of "Sabeel," reminded me of some of those moral issues that my father always brought up in those early years before 1967, and which still remain relevant.

It was in one of those speaking sessions at Sabeel, on November 20, 1997, when I was assigned to speak to a group from the Methodist Volunteers in Mission, that I discovered that six of the group were connected to Southwestern University, from which I had graduated in 1954. It was just as much of a surprise for me as it was for them. That was the beginning of my reconnection with Southwestern. Since then I have been to the campus three times, and I was given the opportunity to speak about our situation to the weekly student assembly and to some of the political science classes. It was so exciting to be there for the 50th class reunion. How I missed having Yousef with me on my last visit when I received the Alumni Association Citation of Merit! Yet it was especially gratifying to me that my daughter Dina was able to accompany me for the occasion, and that the friends whom I had met in Jerusalem, and cousins from Texas, were also there. My acceptance speech appears in Appendix IV.

Receiving Citation of Merit award from the President of
Southwestern University, Dr. Jake Schrum

Euphoria of the Peace Process

We had endless arguments about the Declaration of Principles (DOP) between the Palestine Liberation Organization (PLO) and Israel signed on September 13, 1993, known as the Oslo Accords. Families were split, young and old disagreed, and civil society organizations saw matters from different perspectives. Of course, we all wanted peace. But we were not at all sure that those Accords would end the occupation, nor that they could eventually guarantee the inalienable rights of the Palestinians, especially the Right of Return.

After the Madrid Conference in October 1991, while the Palestinian team, headed by the late Dr. Haidar Abdel-Shafi, was still negotiating in Washington, the Oslo accords were being cooked behind closed doors. The way things turned out, it was not a good meal at all. Indeed, as years passed, that meal proved to be poisonous. I am sure Dr. Abdel Shafi and his team would not have made all the concessions that Oslo brought, concessions that turned out to be at the expense of our rights. It was, however, a memorable sight when Palestinian children, in a visually dramatic first step, flooded the Israeli tanks withdrawing from the main towns in the West Bank with roses and olive tree branches. Five years earlier those children had been chasing the soldiers with stones. The sight was hopeful, to say the least; even those who were against the Oslo Accords, or at least apprehensive about them, felt for a moment that peace was almost around the corner. Too bad Israel never appreciated or utilized that historic moment. In any case, it did not last long. Very soon it had turned into another nightmare.

Under the "Gaza and Jericho First" agreement, cities that were miles apart and connected only through Israeli roads were the focus of the initial Israeli military withdawal. The absurdity of it all was ignored as the Palestinian Authority got busy establishing itself in these areas. For a moment all the reservations about the Oslo Accords seemed to disappear. The Palestinians could not help but react with excitement to what seemed, at the time, "liberation from occupation." Many Palestinians from all over the world were suddenly able to come back to their country, and some business people brought great hopes with them by establishing new businesses. Donor agencies supported all sorts of projects, while training in democracy and civil service, as well as empowerment of women and other sectors, was on the rise. In-kind donations, such as cars, flooded the area. This encouraged the Authority to give its employees free cars, which later proved to be a very unwise initiative. With the increasingly lavish life-style, buildings started mushrooming: skyscrapers, hotels and even a casino in Jericho were erected, and an airport was built in Gaza. The impression developed that all was well, when in reality something was very wrong.

It was the Israeli army that remained just around the corner, not the Peace that had been looming in the air since the famous handshake on the White House lawn between Mr. Arafat and Mr. Rabin in September 1993, during President Clinton's term in office. John Whitbeck, an international lawyer who has advised the Palestinian negotiating team, writes the following about the Gaza Jericho first: "*When the Oslo process began in 1993, the state was hidden away like an inconvenient embarrassment. The first post-Oslo agreement, the Gaza/Jericho Withdrawal Agreement signed in Cairo on May 4, 1994 (timed – and rushed to signature – as a birthday present for Hosni Mubarak), which introduced the unfortunate – and continuing – division of the West Bank into Areas "A", "B" and "C", could have been read as conferring implicit legitimacy on the occupation and as effectively renouncing the state which had been proclaimed in 1988."*[4]

I still recall part of that euphoria when my daughter Dina came home from work after the withdrawal of the Israeli tanks from the major Palestinian cities. She insisted that we should all go to Ramallah, where the excitement was really taking place. So along with the grandchildren we joined the crowds visiting the "Taggard Building," named after the British architect who had designed it during the British Mandate. The building, the headquarters of the Israeli military forces in Ramallah, had now been evacuated and replaced by the Palestinian police, only to eventually become the headquarters, or Muqata'a, of the Palestinian Authority. The cells where so many of our Palestinian youth had been incarcerated were now empty. My son Suhail had spent a night there when the army stopped a bus returning from Birzeit University one afternoon and held a number of students for the night. When he was released the next morning his identity card had been lost, and he had to go through a long ordeal to have the Ministry of Interior in Jerusalem issue him a new one. Everybody was checking out those cells, and that open-house seemed like a celebration for a new beginning. I remember my granddaughter Haya commenting on how nice and pleasant the police were. Of course, I explained to her, they were our own Palestinian police. It was very funny when later on she saw some policemen in Jerusalem and asked me whether they were the nice or the naughty ones. They were naughty indeed: it was not long before all this euphoria turned into another nightmare, after the provocative visit of Prime Minister Ariel Sharon to Al-Aqsa

---

4   In a November 1988 meeting in Algiers, the Palestinian National Council declared the independence of the Arab State of Palestine.

Dina and her children at the new premises of the PNA after the
Israeli Withdrawal

mosque. That visit, on September 28, 2000, under the protection of the Jerusalem police, marked the eruption of the second *Intifada*.

Harsh and innovative measures of harassment by the occupation forces worsened and became increasingly absurd as the days went by. People forced to strip down in the open, hands tied behind their backs, blindfolded, under detention on the streets for hours, were normal sights during those times. This process of dehumanizing the Palestinian population actually reflected how immoral the Israeli army had become, as it stooped to measures to which only sick people would resort. If there was any hope for peace, it certainly was eroded. Those measures only added fuel to the already inflamed situation, breeding more hatred and eventually leading to violent resistance to the occupation. Even the late Israeli singer, Yaffa Yarkoni, known as the singer of the wars because she sang patriotic songs behind the soldiers and for the soldiers, reflected at the time, "*When I saw the Palestinians with their hands tied behind their backs, young men, I said, 'It is like what they did to us in the Holocaust. We are a people that lived through the Holocaust. How can we be capable of such things?*" She paid heavily for her dissenting voice. The town of Kfar Yona canceled her Memorial Day performance, and the Union of Performing Artists canceled its evening of tribute to her.

Israel has never been tolerant of anybody who criticizes its policies. Normally it resorts to applying the label of anti-semitism to people who dare speak the truth. It also makes it very hard for its own people to criticize their state. Indeed, dissenters are often shunned as "self-hating Jews." The new historians, a group of Israelis who have challenged traditional versions of Israeli history, including Israel's role in the Palestinian Exodus in 1948, have not had it easy either. Very often they have had to pursue their career outside the country. These new historians include Ilan Pappe, who was one of the first historians to write about the ethnic cleansing of the Palestinians, drawing on mainly Israeli government documents in his research. Miko Peled and his sister Nurit El-Hannan are also amazing examples of Israelis who are trying to set the record straight about the reality of Israel. In his book, *The Son of a General*, Miko Peled "sweeps away the Zionist myths of 1948, the myth of the existential threat of 1967, and the myth of Jewish democracy."[5]

When the voice of someone such as Peled, who is the son of the legendry Israeli general Matti Peled, is raised to join the voice of his late father about the need to end the occupation, it should serve as a wake up call for all Israelis. Miko, like many Palestinians, sees the one state solution as the only option. His sister Nurit's book, *Palestine in Israeli School Books: Ideology and Propaganda in Education*, deals with the influence of textbooks on Israelis, especially when they grow up and serve in the army. Nurit argues that Israelis have internalized the message that Palestinians are a people whose life is dispensable with impunity, and whose numbers have to be diminished. It is ironic that Israel continuously criticizes the curriculum and textbooks of the Palestinian Authority, while what they claim about Palestinian textbooks is true of Israeli textbooks. In fact, Nurit emphasizes the fact that Palestinian textbooks were published under the supervision of the European Union, whereas there is no supervision over the Israeli's.

It is obvious that there are many more voices than before speaking out for the Palestinian cause, and maybe one source of hope can be found in these dissenting Israeli voices. But unfortunately Israel has often succeeded in propagating false images and information about Palestinians, including children. The propaganda gives the impression that Palestinian mothers allow their children to be in harm's way as targets for Israeli snipers. But Palestinian mothers are like all mothers, caring, loving and protective, even more so in the refugee camps. The only career those women have is motherhood— and a full time job it is. But those families in the refugee camps live in a very limited space, so the street is the playground of their children. The Israelis have not only deprived them of their space, but

---

5   http://mikopeled.com/2011/03/30/my-speech-for-palestine-awareness-week-at-sdsu/

have attacked them in their own so-called self-rule areas. Whether in the city, the village or the refugee camp, women and children have not been spared.

One of those women was Rima Tarazi, who was shot in the eye on January 8, 2001 as she sat in her own home. On that morning, the phone did not stop ringing at our house, as people called asking how my sister Rima was. "Why, she is O.K., but her knee is still aching after surgery, and she has to rest," I answered. "Was she out in a demonstration or something"? Now I was becoming curious. "Why all these questions? Did you hear anything?" One of the callers finally told me that the radio had announced that Rima Tarazi was shot in her home. I could not wait to pick up the phone and call my sister in Ramallah. She was at home and fine. We both realized that the reports must have been about the other Rima Tarazi, who was much younger than my sister and married to Emile Tarazi, a dentist and a cousin of my sister's late husband Antone Tarazi. Then all the details flooded in. The younger Rima, 40 years old, was actually in her home in Dahyiat El-Barid, a housing project in Beit Hanina, up the hill from the checkpoint between Ramallah and Jerusalem. Rima had heard shots coming from the main road, and went to the window to pull down the shutters when a sniper's bullet hit the window and shrapnel went through her eye. She underwent three operations, first to stop the bleeding and then to fix the retina. But I do not think that Rima's eye was ever restored completely. However, she was ever so grateful that she was spared a bullet in the head, as that could have been fatal.

Rima was certainly luckier than Arij Jabali, an 18 year old woman from Hebron. Arij was sitting with her sister-in-law on the porch in their home when a bullet coming from the direction of Beit Haji settlement, in the Hebron area, hit her straight in the chest. All efforts to save her life failed. We have a saying in Arabic that before you rent a house you should ensure you have good neighbors. With the Israeli settlers as neighbors, life in the Hebron area is actual

Shaden Abu Hijleh with her daughter Lana's family

hell. But the Hebronites did not choose their neighbors; it was the settlers who forced themselves in their midst to make the life of the Palestinian residents unbearable. Another young woman, Fatimah Abu Jeish, 20 years old, was shot dead in the back by soldiers in El-Bireh as she was minding her own business. She was the only bread-winner in a family of nine sisters who had lost their father a year before.

When a Palestinian who has not been involved in a confrontation with the settlers or army gets hurt, the Israeli army claims that they had to resort to shooting because they were being attacked. But this has become an old story, one that cannot continue to justify all the bloodshed. The people of Hebron will long remember the massacre at the *Ibrahimi Haram*, when Baruch Goldstein, a Jewish settler, attacked unarmed Muslim worshippers at the mosque during the *Ramadan* prayers on February 25, 1994, killing 29 men and wounding 125.

Similarly, the shooting of Shaden Abu-Hijleh on October 11, 2002, while she was sitting peacefully on her porch embroidering, was absolutely murder in cold blood. On that day I was sitting in the hospital, accompanying my husband during his second chemotherapy session. I was reading in the newspaper about the sniper who had been terrorizing the Washington area. It was not surprising to read that the residents of the area were petrified to move around. Yet I could not help but wonder about the effect of all the violent movies produced in the USA on people, including the violent cartoons that are shown on TV and somehow end up being stories in real life.

In the meantime my daughter Dina came in to see us. She signaled to me in a way that only women can understand, and we both left the room. Whatever she wanted to tell me, I knew she did not want her father to know. She broke the sad news of the deadly shooting of Shaden. Shaden's husband and son had also been on the porch with her when an Israeli jeep stopped in front of their house and, without any provocation, started shooting. Luckily the men were spared, except for slight injuries. Shaden was the maternal grandmother of our granddaughter Zeina, and I had been at her home so many times. She was a very active woman and a gracious hostess. I was sure it would never be the same at the Abu Hijleh's residence after Shaden's murder.

Two days later my sister-in-law Tania's mother, who was over 90 years old, passed away in her sleep, and a cousin of my father, Aunt Karimeh, who was almost as old, passed away peacefully at an old-age home run by the German nuns at Qubeibeh. It is indeed a blessing to die in bed these days. The brutality of the occupation has made a peaceful death to Palestinians a privilege. But very often the Israelis themselves have not been spared, because they refuse to accept the fact that their own living and dying in peace cannot be realized so long as they are depriving an entire population of their basic right to live freely and die peacefully.

A couple of months after the eruption of the second *Intifada*, it was time for the olive harvest. Olive oil and olives are staple foods for Palestinians, rich, or poor, professional, or laborer, all eat olives with every meal at their dining tables. Of course for some it is a whole meal by itself. I still remember when we were children how much we enjoyed tagging along with the older cousins of the family during the olive harvesting season. Not that we were able to do much, but it was simply the joy of being part of a cooperative endeavor in which all the villagers, young and old, gathered to pick their olives together. But in 2000 the festive annual olive picking time turned into a bloody season. Since then it has remained a nightmare, as settlers continue to raid olive groves, burn trees, and prevent farmers from reaching their land. In Beit Fourik, in the Nablus area that same year, two armed settlers from the settlement of Itmar, which had been built on confiscated land from Beit Fourik, attacked the villagers and started shooting at random. Hamdi Issa was saved by the sack of olives he was carrying, as the bullet went through it before it injured him, turning the sack into a bloody bundle. Farid Nassasrah (28) was not as lucky, as he was fatally shot, while Khaled Issa (34) and Malek Nassasrah (33) were both wounded and needed hospitalization.

As if all the raids and shootings were not enough, the Israeli soldiers at the checkpoint were continuously conniving more innovative means to harass the people whose livelihoods depended on the olive harvest. At the village of Boureen, also in the Nablus area, a villager who was hauling thirty 20-litre cans of olive oil was stopped at a checkpoint that was manned by settlers alongside the Israeli soldiers. He was asked to curse Prophet Mohammad so as to be allowed to pass through. When he refused, they started pouring out his oil, one can after the other. Because he insisted on not complying with their request, he left the checkpoint without his oil.

The next morning, he found 25 cans of olive oil at his doorstep. The solidarity and unity of the Palestinians at that time compensated for personal loss, and enabled people to resist and overcome brutality. In another incident, a woman was forced to kiss all the passengers in the taxi so that they would be allowed to go through. In yet another incident, a group of students were forced to break their fast during the holy month of Ramadan so as to be able to cross the checkpoint. The stories are endless.

In the meantime, at the Sharm El-Sheikh second Summit on October 17, 2000, both Ehud Barak and Yasser Arafat agreed to issue public statements unequivocally calling for an end of violence. But while Israel arrogantly insisted that the Palestinian Authority should abide by the summit agreement and stop the violence, soon after the summit Israel hit Beit Jala, a Palestinian town near Bethlehem, with a rocket, and killed ten Palestinians across the country. In Askar, on the outskirts of Nablus, on Thursday, October 19, a group of settlers claimed to be going out for a walk to have a look at Joseph's Tomb. That "innocent" walk brought about a bloody evening as the settlers opened fire on the olive pickers, shooting dead 37-year-old Zahi Fathi El-Adda. Palestinian Security came to the rescue of the defenseless people of Askar, while the Israeli army started shelling the area from Mount Gerizim, in Nablus, with the support of helicopters. An Israeli settler was killed and around fifteen Palestinians were injured. All this took place after the Israeli military claimed that it had withdrawn its troops from the outskirts of Nablus. It continues to be crystal clear that the violence can only come to an end when the Israeli occupation itself comes to an end.

The American Congress, in the meantime, threatened to pass a law withholding aid to the Palestinian Authority until it complied with the Sharm el-Sheikh summit agreement. How ironic. For the last 33 years Israel has refused to comply with any UN resolutions, especially Resolutions 242 and 338, which stipulate the withdrawal from the Territories Israel occupied in 1967. Yet the American administration sees fit to reward Israel with moral and financial support for its disobedience and its non-compliance with UN resolutions. It seems that the more Israel oppresses the Palestinians, the more the US supplies it with sophisticated arms to ensure "Israel's security." That is the lopsided logic of US policy and Israel.

One would think that at least on solemn occasions such as Yom Kippur, a time for atonement, or the memorial of Kristallnacht, the Jews would take time out to be at peace with themselves and to ponder how this occupation has dehumanized them. They had vowed "Never Again," and rightly so, "Never Again." But it should never happen again to anyone, neither to Jews, nor Christians, nor Muslims, nor Israelis, nor Palestinians. Yet on the eve of Yom Kippur, October 9, 2000, a day of prayer and fasting, one of the holiest days for the Jewish people, Israeli settlers rampaged our area in Beit Hanina adjacent to the Neve Yacov settlement. They attacked some of the houses and the church down the hill from our house. Luckily, we were spared, but our neighbors were not, and we all had the scare of our life. The children kept waking up petrified all night long, while all the residents stayed on watch till the early hours of the morning. Those settlers and the Israeli government will certainly need more than just one day of atonement for their actions!

It was not any better on November 9, 2000, the eve of the commemoration of Khristallnacht. On this night of November 9, 1938, the Nazis unleashed a wave of pogroms against German Jews, damaging and destroying homes, synagogues, businesses, etc. In Palestine on November 9, 2000, in the Shepherds' Field near Beit Sahour in the Bethlehem area, where the angels brought the good tidings to the shepherds two thousand years ago, there was another Kristallnacht. The Israeli Army launched an assault on an unarmed civilian population. Buildings, houses, clubs, factories, a theatre and a church were all attacked. The pogroms spread to Beit Jala in the Bethlehem area, Ramallah, Jenin, and Gaza, with attacks by helicopter and missiles. A direct hit on a car in Beit Sahour killed one of the Fatah leaders and injured ten other people.

On October 15, 2000, hell broke loose after the lynching of two Israelis in Ramallah. It turned out they were under-cover soldiers who were driving a car with Palestinian license plates (a fact that definitely negated the claim that they were innocent Israelis who had gotten lost in Ramallah). They must have had a hidden agenda, because they panicked when they were spotted. However, the lynching was a very ugly and brutal sight. As sad as it was, it must have been a reaction to all the brutality that the Palestinians have been subjected to during the long years of occupation. The police station where the lynching took place was very close to the Friends Boys School, where our oldest grandson, Omar, was enrolled. Israel was threatening to bomb certain targets, including the police station. Everybody panicked, and parents rushed to the school to pick up their children.

A friend of Omar's father offered to take the boy to Birzeit, where his father was teaching at the time, so Omar went with them. My friend Cedar had picked up my other three grandchildren, Haya, Zeina and Faress, along with her grand-daughter Juman, from the Friends Girls School, which was also in Ramallah. In the meantime, Amal Duaibis, Cedar's daughter, stopped by the Boys School to pick up Omar. When they did not find him, Haya, his ten-year old sister, panicked and had a hysterical fit, thinking for sure that he had been taken away by the army. Had they had the cell phones we have nowadays, they all could have been spared the trauma. Eventually Amal arrived safely with the children to Beit Hanina. Omar found his father at the university, but they could not come to Beit Hanina. All the towns were under siege. Dina was able to get to Ramallah the next day simply because she had a UN car. She was still working with UNRWA at the time as Field Nursing Officer. As it was almost impossible to get either in or out of Jerusalem, people were trying to find roundabout ways to get to their destinations, even if they had to use rough or dirt roads.

During that same week a young Palestinian from Um-Safa, north of Birzeit, who was on his way to paint the gate of the village

cemetery, was lynched by Israeli settlers. According to an eye-
Witness he was picked up by the army, and the next day he was
found killed near the settlement of Halmish in that area. He had
been tortured and burnt to death. There was no camera on site, so
that story was not publicized around the world as was the killing of
the two Israeli soldiers in Ramallah. But the story was known to all
in the area, and the young man's photos and medical report were
circulated on the internet by human rights activists.

It was very sad and frustrating that while President Clinton
was very quick to condemn the killing of the Israeli soldiers, he
did not condemn the bombing of Palestinian targets. So once again
the US demanded that Mr. Arafat put an end to violence, without
any reference to the violence of the Israeli forces or settlers. But
then, the double standard by which the US government deals with
issues pertaining to Israel and Palestine, and the way in which it
treats Israel as if it is above the law, was not new. Unforuntately, this
double standard has certainly not helped in the progress of the Peace
Process.

Despite Israel's peace rhetoric, I have my doubts that Israel
is serious or genuine about achieving peace. All that has been
happening actually indicates that Israel cannot survive in times of
peace. Given all the internal political conflicts amongst the various
Israeli political and religious parties, as well as Israel's various ethnic
groups, which Uri Avnery, an Israeli peace activist and writer, refers
to in his weekly article of January 21, 2012, as "blockbusters," it
seems to me that Israel will always need a common enemy to be able
to cope with its diverse population and to maintain internal peace
amongst its own people. Indeed, it seems that every time there is a
general feeling that peace with the Palestinians is about to be forged,
the Israeli government creates a new crisis to evade peace, and to
divert the attention of the whole world to the new crisis.

This time it was Sharon, head of the opposition party, Likud,
who was brought on to create the crisis. But the crisis spiraled

out of control, like Pandora's box, providing the Israeli Arabs[6] the opportunity to express their disenchantment with the government for not responding to their grievances. It is worth noting that Israeli Arabs have been struggling for equal rights since the establishment of the state in 1948. Struggling for one's rights and for liberation from occupation is a legitimate struggle for any oppressed people in the world. In the name of security Israel continues to oppress its own citizens as well as the population of the occupied territories. Israel's security has always been its phobia, its obsession, and the phobia of its allies. It is like a thief on the run. Israel gets away with all its violations and illegal land acquisition because it claims that it is forced to take those measures for security reasons. But justice is the only guarantee for security.

If the US administration truly wants the violence to stop, it has to see to it that the root cause of the violence (the occupation) is removed. That is why it sounded so ridiculous when Ben Ami, the Israeli Deputy Foreign Minister, said at one time that Arafat cannot hold the whole world hostage: in fact, it is Israel that has been holding the world hostage. Watching the American elections campaign, and listening to candidates outdo each other to prove themselves more patriotic to Israel, one would think they were running for Israeli, not US, elections. But they were all outdone by the latest candidates for the Republican Party: Newt Gingrich, a historian, who made a laughing stock out of himself by stating that the Palestinians were an invented people, and Senator Santorum, who claimed that the residents of the West Bank were not Palestinians.

While Iraq was forced to withdraw from its occupation of Kuwait in 1991 in no time, and rightly so, the Israeli occupation has been entrenched and maintained with the moral and financial support of the US administration.

---

6 "Israeli Arabs" is the name that Israel gave to the Palestinians who remained in Palestine after the Nakba and the establishment of the state of Israel. The intention was to erase the name "Palestinian" and emphasize "Arab" – implying that they had other Arab countries to go to. It was completely forbidden to use the words "Palestine" or "Palestinian."

Not Another Oslo

Although the Oslo Accords provided for the establishment of a Palestinian National Authority (PNA), interim Palestinian self-government was to be granted by Israel in phases. The PNA was therefore continuously at the mercy of Israel. Meanwhile, Israel was taking advantage of the situation to create new realities on the ground.

It did not take political analysts or geniuses to realize that the negotiations were heading nowhere. With the Israeli elections coming up at the beginning of 2001, both Israel and the US administration were keen on resuming the negotiations which had been interrupted due to the failure of the Camp David summit in July 2000 and the eruption in September 2000 of the second *Intifada*, known as the Al-Aqsa *Intifada*. But a conflict that has lingered for over half a century cannot be solved in a few months to suit the desires of politicians, whether Mr. Barak's political campaign goals or Mr. Clinton's wish to gain credit for forging peace in the Middle East before his term officially ended.

I could not help but wonder at how much hope we Palestinians attach to elections. Every time there are elections in the US, we hope that the policy toward the Middle East will change. And every time there are elections in Israel, we hope that a government will come into power there that will have the courage to redress the injustice that has been inflicted upon us. Yet whether it is the Democrats or the Republicans in the US or the Likud, Labor or Kadima in Israel, we are forced to realize that they are all the same where Palestine is concerned. The end result is that we continue to be dispossessed of our rights.

In 1996 we finally had our own first elections in preparation for the statehood that was to come about in the last stages of the Oslo Accords. I remember how excited I was to be able to vote for the first time in my life. I even took along my camera and had my husband take a photo of me putting my ballot in the box, for fear I would not have this opportunity again. But in retrospect, maybe it was a mistake to have elections or cabinet ministers while we were still under occupation. Maybe a few coordinators for basic services would have been enough.

Samia casting her vote during the first elections

The "Gaza and Jericho First" agreement signed on May 4, 1994, a follow-up to the Oslo Accords intended to provide autonomy to those areas, proved to be an absurdity. The two areas included in the agreement were on opposite sides of the Palestinian map and completely disconnected. Furthermore, as a result of the agreement, both areas became out of bounds for us Jerusalemites; we needed permits to get into any of those areas. I still recall how difficult it was for me to get to Gaza to offer condolences to the Tarazi family when my sister's sister-in-law passed away in summer of 2000.

As a result of the changes brought by the agreement, when the YWCA of Jericho invited us to attend their annual bazaar it had to secure permits for us to enter the area. But shortly before heading to Jericho, we received a telephone call from the YWCA, informing us that all permits had been cancelled. We were advised to come through a back route, Wadi El-Qilt, a rough and narrow road that had no checkpoints.

Jane Wolfe, the World YWCA president at that time, was with us, as we had all just come back from the YWCA regional meeting for the Middle East in Amman, Jordan. Ironically, crossing the bridge to Amman and then back again to Jerusalem, which used to be a nightmare, was much smoother that time than our trip to Jericho. On the road to Jericho we had to climb out of the car twice as the driver struggled to maneuver along a very steep and bumpy road. As we finally approached Jericho, the driver made it clear to us that it would not be possible to go back the same way, because the car would not make it up the hill. But with the excitement of seeing so many of our old friends in Jericho, and the lovely display of the food products, embroidery and other handicrafts, we simply dismissed the worry about the trip back to Jerusalem.

It was beautiful to see all the community of Jericho involved in the bazaar and supportive of the YWCA. But as usual, we were not privileged to have good things last for long. Shortly after the opening of the Bazaar, we got word that the Israelis were shelling the Headquarters of the Palestinian Security Forces in Jericho. At times like these, one cannot but reflect on the effects of what seemed to be a false peace process. The words of Lord Chesterfield to his son were so pertinent at that moment: "Go to the bottom of things. Anything half done, or half known, is neither done nor known at all. Nay, worse, for it often misleads." The Oslo Accords didn't end the occupation. Yet they gave a false impression that we were liberated. During the pre-Oslo era, we were at least one entity, and we did not need permits to drive for hours through checkpoints. All Palestinians had access to Jerusalem as well as to the Palestinian towns that became part of Israel after 1948. After Oslo, none of that was true. As much as we had hoped that the peace process would truly liberate us, it was clear that because it was not done fully and honestly, nor thoroughly or completely, it ended up making us hostages of a process that brought neither peace, nor liberation, nor security to the region.

Irrespective of my reflections, we eventually had to think about how we would get back to Jerusalem. Going through the checkpoint would raise the question of how we got in. The story of Joyce Nasir with two of her friends two days earlier was still fresh in our minds. When they were denied entry to Jericho, they went through the same rough road of Wadi El-Qilt that we took, but returned from the regular entrance through the checkpoint. Because they had entered "illegally," their identity card numbers were registered on a blacklist, and the Israeli military forces told them that they would not be allowed into Jericho again. And this is an area that is supposedly Palestinian, from which the Israeli army had withdrawn! Of course, the military forces might have been "pulling a good one" on them, but we did not want to risk anything, and so we had to look for an alternative. We eventually found a way out through another dirt road, El-Oujah, which connected to the main road without passing through a checkpoint.

We finally arrived, safe at last, but were so drained that we could not even enjoy the savories that we had brought back with us.

At the time it seemed like the US administration and the whole international community were urging the Palestinians not to miss what was presented as a great opportunity for peace. But then, we have always been threatened that we should not miss the boat, or the train, and as a result we have always ended up on a sinking boat, or a crashing train. "Missed opportunities," as Israel and the US administration call them, were simply part of the Israeli disinformation plan to discredit the Palestinians as peace partners. The reality is that the only choice we have ever had is between a bad offer and a worse offer. The bad offers started with the partition scheme of Palestine in 1948, a glaring injustice of a plan that allocated 56% of the land to a Jewish minority who were only 32.5% of the population and who owned only 5.6% of the land by purchase. As years passed, the bad offers eventually brought us to Ehud Barak's "generous offer at Camp David," whereby Israel would return only 88% of the Occupied Territories of 1967, which are themselves only 22% of historic Palestine. Barak's "generous offer" would also have annexed big chunks of the West Bank and Jerusalem, fragmented the country into four cantons, and denied the right of return of Palestinian refugees. This plan, which Mr. Arafat completely refused, was in no way a generous offer. As if the humiliation of that offer was not enough, later on the Palestinian Authority was also forced to consider land swaps "for the sake of peace." These were presented as if the Palestinians had had all of Palestine restored to them, and as if peace was dependent only on a swap of territory that the Palestinians did not even control. But then, that is part of the absurd logic of military occupation. (At the time, I wrote an open letter to Mr. Arafat. A copy appears in Appendix V.)

During the Israeli elections campaign the opposition – the Likud party – announced clearly that it would not be obliged to adhere to any agreements arrived at by the Labor party. In the meantime, Mr. Olmert, the mayor of Jerusalem, decided to move his office for a week to the area in the middle of Jerusalem off the Wailing Wall, also known as the Western Wall, Judaism's holiest site. Olmert was asked on Israeli TV whether such an action would not be considered another provocative move, comparable to the Sharon visit in September 2000 to the area of Haram El-Sharif, the Muslim holy site in Jerusalem that Israel claims as the site of the destroyed Jewish Temple, which sparked the second *Intifada*. Olmert responded arrogantly that he was the Mayor of the United Eternal Capital of Israel, and he would do as he chose; neither Arafat nor Saib Ureiqat (the chief Palestinian negotiator) could dictate what he should do.

Mr. Barak lost the elections on February 6, 2001 despite his peace campaign, and Ariel Sharon was elected. The election of Sharon was bad news for Palestinians, and bad news, too, for the Israeli peace camp, just as the 1996 election of Netanyahu had been.

By electing Sharon and bringing the Likud party to power, the Israelis said loudly and clearly, "No Peace." Perhaps one of the core myths of Israel was thus exposed: Israel did not crave or seek peace. Whoever nicknamed Sharon a bulldozer must have known him very well: a bulldozer he truly was, until a stroke stopped him. He was known not only for his atrocities and his criminal past, but also for being a "fait accompli" man who never failed to create a new reality or to use innovative means to kill Palestinians or drive them out. (One of my high school classmates, Musa Abu-Zeid, was Sharon's victim during the Qibyeh massacre in 1953. In this massacre, Israeli troops, under Sharon, attacked the village of Qibyeh in the West Bank and killed 69 Palestinians, two thirds of them women and children.) Through his actions, Sharon dehumanized not only himself but also his own soldiers. It is worth remembering that Sharon never approved of the Oslo Accords.

Sharon used to claim that he had no problem with the Palestinian people; his problem was with the Palestinian leadership. Very often we too feel that our problem is with the Palestinian leadership, for being too accommodating to Israel. Despite good faith and yearning for peace, the Palestinian leadership has made too many concessions, including forfeiting its right to 78% of historic Palestine. And what

Women in Black at their weekly protest.

has Israel offered as a peace gesture? A separation wall. Indeed, it exerts its brutality not only against the Palestinians but also against its own peace activists, such as Neta Golan, who was beaten by Israeli police at a non-violent demonstration and whose arm was twisted to the point of fracture by her own country's forces.

It is ironic that upon the election of Sharon we did not hear the same rage and uproar that erupted when the right wing Austrian Haider was elected as chairman of the Freedom Party of Austria (FPO), a far right political party. On the contrary, Mr. George W. Bush was the first one to congratulate Sharon. Naturally, following his master's lead, the British Prime Minister Tony Blair was quick to also offer his congratulations. Once again the world community proved to have one set of rules for the whole world and a different, special set of rules for Israel.

Yet I never lost hope that there is a way to reach the world conscience, to create a better world that would make Mother Earth a true haven for future generations. The Israeli soldiers who are serving sentences in Israeli jails for refusing to serve in the Occupied

Territories, such as Gabi Wolfe and reservist Ishai Rozen-Zvi; the protests against the occupation and against the closures by Israeli members of Women in Black[7]; and the courageous actions of peace activists such as Neta Golan, could be signs of that hope. Although these young men and women, so greatly appreciated and recognized by the Palestinians, have not been able to make a dent in Israeli policy, it is extremely important that their voices continue to be heard loudly and clearly. Through their protests and their actions they refute the narrative of the Israeli government, which has led its people to believe that their security can only be guaranteed with an iron fist and through the acquisition of more and more land, in an indefinite stretching of Israel's borders. It is ironic that although Israel has never defined its borders, it nonetheless continuously demands a secure border, and proclaims its right to defend this undefined border.

I recall one ordinary Sunday morning. I started the day by checking my e-mail. By the time I was finished reading about all the brutality of the Israeli forces, including violence against Palestinian children, I did not have the stomach to go to church. I thought of my friend Linda, the wife of a Presbyterian pastor, whom I had met at the Presbyterian women's assembly at Purdue in 1985. During the Gulf War, she wrote to me one Sunday morning to tell me that she had opted not to go to church, but instead to sit and share her worries with me. Her two sons were in the American Air Force. What if she had lost those boys in Iraq? For whom were they really fighting in that war? I could feel her pain through her letters and in our telephone conversations. Thank heavens, her sons were spared. But the suffering throughout the Middle East region continues.

In our science and math classes in school we were taught that

---

7 Women in Black are part of a world-wide network of women committed to peace with justice and actively opposed to injustice, war, militarism and other forms of violence. Women in Black chapters focus on challenging the militarist policies of their own governments. The Israeli chapter of Women in Black holds a vigil every Friday noon at Hagar Square in Jerusalem, holding signs written in Hebrew, Arabic, and English protesting the military occupation.

the shortest distance between two points is a straight line. And in the gospel, Mark 1:3, we hear, "A voice of one calling in the desert, prepare the way for the Lord, make straight paths for him." Unfortunately, however, politicians do not walk that straight path; they zigzag so much that their path never leads anywhere, let alone to the necessary destination. This zigzagging has defined Palestinian history. In the *Nakba* of 1948, Palestinians were evicted by Jewish militias at gunpoint or fled their homes out of fear. All the UN resolutions that ensued could not redress that grave injustice of the Palestinian dispossession, because there was no will to enforce them. But in 1967, when Israel occupied the rest of the Palestinian territories, a new reality was created. Instead of moving in a straight line from problem to solution, the politicians zigzagged: now there was a new reality to deal with, as if 1967 was the starting point of our dispossession. Soon after, East Jerusalem was unilaterally and illegally annexed to Israel, and we had another new reality: the illegal annexation of Jerusalem. In the meantime, Israel implemented whatever laws it wished to implement, and declared Jerusalem "The united eternal capital of Israel," defying international law and United Nations resolutions. And all this time, the intense wave of illegal Jewish colonies, or settlements, continued to carve up the landscape of the newly occupied territories of Palestine, redrawing the map and complicating the straight line from problem to solution. These illegal colonies popped up on hilltops, on land that had been confiscated from its owners. The settlements thus became the latest issue that we needed to deal with. According to the US administration, they were an "obstacle to peace." But no one took action to remove that obstacle, and the settlements kept mushrooming.

The injustice and consequences of our *Nakba* and the violations against our political rights continue to be minimized at every stage and with every new "fait-accompli." When we finally had enough, and protested loudly and clearly through the *Al-Aqsa Intifada*, we were blessed with a variety of missions and envoys demanding that we "stop the violence."

Indeed, the Palestine Question and the repeated violations of our inalienable human rights have been watered down along the years to this distorted view: that the Palestinians need to "stop the violence." Even the UN Secretary General, who has failed to ensure that any of the UN resolutions regarding Palestinian rights were implemented, found himself caught in this zigzag, beat-around-the-bush diplomacy. Thus, he demanded that the Israelis and Palestinians implement the Mitchell Report and the Tenet Document[8], as if Palestinians and Israelis had equal power and equal responsibility for the situation. At the time I thought that all those envoys would be better off staying home unless they had something honorable to offer, and most importantly unless they had the power and the will to implement the numerous United Nations resolutions passed over the years which had never been put into practice. We'd had enough crumbs over the last fifty three years.

Thinking about how the focus on the basic issue had been so lost, I found myself thinking about the Taliban's decree, in February 2001, that the ancient Buddhist relics in Afghanistan should be destroyed. I almost wished that the Palestinians could have been those statues. The Taliban's decree focused the attention of the world on the relics, and the international community chivalrously rallied to salvage those important monuments. Personally, I had no problem with the issue. I actually signed a petition against the destruction of the statues, for one's cultural heritage, whether stones or not, is a precious thing to hold on to. The Taliban who destroyed the Buddhist relics in Afghanistan are seen by the world community as a benighted people, and perhaps no one should expect better of them. But Israel is considered by the Western world to be "civilized," the "only democracy in the Middle East."

---

8 The Mitchell Report was a document produced by an American fact-finding committee, led by former US Senator George J. Mitchell, at the early stages of the Al-Aqsa Intifada. The Tenet Plan was an Israeli-Palestinian ceasefire and security plan proposed by then Central Inteligence Agency (CIA) Director George Tenet.

It hurt that there was never the same urgency and resolve in world opinion to salvage the *living stones* of Palestine: the Palestinian people. Perhaps the first time that the world listened to those living Palestinian stones was when the sound of real stones was heard during the first *Intifada* in 1987. Stones in Palestine are very much part of the landscape. We build our houses with stone, we terrace our fields and groves with stone, we crush our olives in preparation for pickling with stone, and children use stones for a variety of games, such as hopscotch and jacks. So perhaps it was no surprise that in 1987 Palestinian children resorted to stones, the only means available to them, to resist an occupation that had already prevailed for twenty years. The silence was too loud. "I tell you, if they keep quiet, the stones will cry out" (Luke 19:40). Are not Palestinians as important as stones? Is the Israeli occupation not destroying every aspect of Palestinian life?

Two of the many stories that touched my heart deeply during these long years of Israeli military occupation were the stories of Dr. Nurit Peled–Elhanan and of Ismail El-Khatib. Nurit is an Israeli Jewish woman whose only daughter, Smadar, 13 years old, was killed in September 1997 in Jerusalem by a suicide bomber. Ismail is a Palestinian Muslim whose 12-year old son, Ahmad, was shot by the Israeli army in Jenin in November 2005, on the morning of "Eid el-Fitr," the Muslim holiday after the month of fasting. One child was killed by an individual act of violence, by a representative of a Palestinian group resisting Israeli occupation, while the other child was killed by the occupying military forces of the State of Israel. Of course, the world looks at the violence on the part of resistance movements struggling for liberation and independence as "terrorism," while state violence on behalf of the occupiers is always justified for the security of the state. I was inspired by Israeli security phobia that I wrote an Ode to Security which was published in my book "A Rhyme for Every Time." See Appendix VI.

When Nurit was asked by a reporter why she was willing to accept condolences from "the other side," she explained that the other side – the enemy – was not the Palestinian people, and that the struggle is between those who seek peace and those who seek war. That is why when representatives of Netanyahu's government came to offer Nurit their condolences she would not sit with them. In her speech to Women in Black she said: "My people are those who seek peace. My sisters are the bereaved mothers, Israeli and Palestinian, who live in Israel and in Gaza and in the refugee camps. My brothers are those fathers who try to defend their children from the cruel occupation, and are, as I was, unsuccessful in doing so."

Despite her great loss, Nurit did not become a bitter woman. She was able to see clearly the root cause of the "terror" that claimed the life of her daughter. The Israeli military occupation was the enemy, and that is why she continues to speak out in order to spare other mothers, both Palestinian and Israeli, the traumatic experience that she went through.

Similarly, Ismail Khatib reacted to the loss of his child by donating his son's organs to the Israeli hospital where Ahmad was taken after he was shot. It would have been very easy for him not to even think of such a detail in the midst of his sorrow, but he did not lose focus, especially when he was comforted by Zvi Frankental, an Israeli whose own son had been killed by Hamas. Out of this sad experience Ismail wanted to spare other parents the experience of losing a child: an option made available to him only by the loss of his own child.

Never a Dull Moment

Living under a military occupation, one can be sure there will never be a dull moment. Even when a day starts normally, there is always the unexpected popping up at you.

My heart goes out to my grandchildren and so many of their age group who do not have any notion what the future holds for them. So many children have been victim of the violence of occupation: those who were shot to death, or those who continue to struggle to stay alive and claim a normal childhood despite the abnormal situation, despite being deprived of dreaming about our future.

I continually recognize how blessed I am in so many ways. With our two children and their families living on the same property, our grandchildren are fortunate to have most of their cousins living in the same neighborhood. They have been able to visit each other regularly, even during those very difficult times of the second *Intifada* when getting around was not easy. But they too have felt the pressures of occupation. I recall a Sunday morning in March 2001. I was relaxing and reading the morning paper before getting ready for church. Our ten-year old granddaughter, Haya, asked me to give her a ride; she wanted to go and help our niece bake a cake for her daughter's birthday. Our niece lived just around the corner, and Haya's request to drive her one hundred meters would, under normal circumstances, have sounded ridiculous. But I immediately understood why she did not want to walk that short path alone. I put on my robe and slippers and drove her.

I knew Haya asked me to drive her because of a news report we had watched the night before. A ten-year-old Palestinian boy, exactly Haya's age, had been found killed, his head bashed in, in the Israeli settlement of Neve Ya'acov, adjacent to our residential area. The boy had been missing for two days, and the Israeli police had made no effort to respond to the request of the parents to search for him. Eventually it was the family who found him in a small forest between his neighborhood, Dahiyat El-Bared, and the Neve Ya'acov settlement, where he often used to play with his friends. Such violence, especially against a child, is beyond comprehension. Haya and her brothers had seen how horrified we were while watching the news. It was no surprise that she was scared of walking alone, even for a short distance in daylight. On my way back I wondered what future awaits her and the rest of her generation.

The four-year-old birthday girl, Sama, whom Haya wanted to help bake a cake for, was my sister Rima's first grandchild. She was born on March 17, 1997, shortly before her grandfather died, so she has been Rima's great consolation. Sama feels equally attached to her grandmother. The best treat for Sama is to spend the night with *Teta* (grandma). They sit and listen to music for hours. I have never seen another child who could watch a whole opera in one sitting before she was even three. And of course she skips and dances to music as well. It is very clear that some of Rima's musical genes must have been passed on to Sama. I remember when we were teenagers living in Upper Baka'a in Jerusalem before 1948, and my mother used to assign household chores to us, Rima's favorite chore was to dust the living room, because she could do that while dancing and skipping to music. Watching her through his window, our elderly neighbor thought she was the house help, and asked my mother if she would be willing to let her clean his house for him. It was the joke of the neighborhood at the time. Little did he know how much Rima hated to do the dirty work. When it was her turn to clean the bathroom, she would often offer to make my bed for a whole week, if I would only relieve her of that chore. With the closures between Jerusalem and Ramallah, Sama was miserable, because she was deprived of her *Teta*. She could not understand why she could not go to see her, or why *Teta* could not come over for her birthday. "The area is closed," her mother tried to explain. "Who closed it?" Sama wanted to know. "It is simply closed," her mother answered, thinking that was the end of the story, and that there was no need to expand on the issue of soldiers and occupation to a four year old. But when Sama insisted on knowing who closed that road, her mother gave in and explained that it was the soldiers, and that there was no way for anybody to go through. Little Sama grasped all that, because she already sensed that anything to do with soldiers must be serious. After a long silence, she came to her mother and said, "You know, I think I will go buy a gun to get rid of those soldiers, so I can go see *Teta*." Many birthdays were celebrated without *Teta*, but Sama learned how to cope by ignoring the soldiers and their guns and going on with life, crossing the checkpoint daily to go to the Friends School in Ramallah. She fulfilled her musical dream, and that of her grandmother, when she became one of the young musicians in the Palestine Youth Orchestra of the Edward Said National Conservatory of Music[9]. She was also part of the Palestine Strings of the Conservatory, which toured in the US in summer 2010 and performed at the BBC promps in London in summer 2013. Her latest experience after the Italian tour of the Palestine Youth Orchestera in July 2012 was to perform in London with three other Palestinian musicians as part of the 2012 British Council/Choir of London Bursary Scheme.

---

9 The National Conservatory of Music was founded in 1993 by five Palestinian musicians and music teachers, under the auspices of Birzeit University. In 2004, as a tribute to Palestinian scholar and musician Edward Said, the conservatory changed its name to the Edward Said National Conservatory of Music. The Conservatory now has five branches—in Ramallah, Jerusalem, Bethlehem, Nablus and Gaza—an outreach program, four orchestras, a variety of ensembles, and a wind band.

Sama on the right of the front row with the Palestine Strings

Sama's great grandmother, Aunt Evelyn Baramki, my mother's sister, was the last living family member of her generation who had Witnessed both the *Nakba* of 1948 as well as the occupation of the rest of Palestine in 1967. Aunt Evelyn was already 95 years old when the second *Intifada* broke out. I still remember celebrating her 90th birthday. With her beautiful voice, she led us through some of her favorite songs in Arabic, English and French. One of the songs she sang in a duet with her son Gabi was "Darling, I am Growing Old," a song she used to sing for him when he was a child. It was a beautiful performance.

Shortly after Sama's birthday, on March 28, 2001, the Baramkis called to say that dear old aunt Evelyn had passed away at the hospital. With her pleasant, happy go lucky personality, she had been ready for her eternal trip for years. One time, as she was complaining that it was really time to go, her grandson Toni (Nadim), who has a dry sense of humor, suggested that she should consider keeping her bedroom window open at night in order to catch pneumonia,

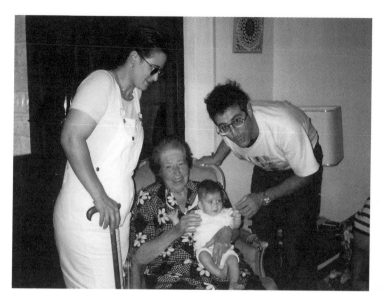

Sama with her great grandmother Evlyne and her parents Marwan and Ranya

which was bound to be fatal at her age! But it was really a blessing to have her around the children and grandchildren, who so enjoyed her singing and stories, most of which she made up on the spot.

As I broke the news about Aunt Evelyn to my husband that morning, I realized that we were on the front line now. Evelyn's daughter, Laura, is not only my cousin, but my sister-in-law as well, and her son George is married to Yousef's sister. So the whole family was affected by her passing. We all gathered at the Baramkis residence in Ramallah the evening before the funeral. My sister Rima had to leave us to go to the Grand Park Hotel, where she and my son Suhail had a dinner meeting with a Swedish group regarding the Edward Said National Conservatory of Music. (Rima is one of the Conservatory's founders, and the chairperson of its supervisory board. And Suhail is general director of the Conservatory, which has been contributing to the cultural landscape of the Palestinian community for years.)

My brother Hanna and his wife Tania left early, as they were anxious not to be out late on the road to Birzeit. And then, the unexpected happened in Ramallah. Rima called to say that she and Suhail and the Swedish group were in the basement of the hotel, because the Israelis were shelling the nearby area. The next telephone call was from our daughter, Dina, who had heard the news about the shelling and was extremely worried.. The telephone never stopped ringing, as all the children took it in turns to check on their parents, who were all gathered at the Baramkis. The electricity had been cut off in Beit Hanina. We were all very anxious that further shelling might take place, and that we would not be able to get back home. Or worse yet, we were worried that the settlers from the neighboring settlement were going to go on a rampage, as they had done at the beginning of the *Intifada*. Some of us really panicked, others were very anxious, and yet others were very calm and relaxed. I was absolutely numb, wondering what it would be like if the shelling started again while we were at the funeral the next day, as the cemetery is very close to the area that had been shelled.

We finally made it home, driving in a convoy. Thanks to the mobile phones which some of the cousins had, we kept in touch until we all reached our homes safely. Suhail eventually accompanied the Swedish group to their hotel in Jerusalem. They had had the scare of their lives as they experienced all that shelling. In retrospect, after everybody was safe, we thought that we should consider it as part of our Palestinian hospitality to share even our personal experiences of occupation and shelling with our guests! It was a real live sound and light show.

That evening, I remembered that when I wrote to our cousins, in May 1996, to invite them to join us in celebrating Aunt Evelyn's 90th birthday, I had specifically mentioned that planning ahead does not mean much, because under occupation the unexpected is always bound to happen. And it did happen on the day she passed away. Bless her soul. But at least she had a decent funeral, not like 68 year old Jamil Mattar, who had died a few days before her. Jamil had been struggling with a terminal disease, and had been hospitalized in Egypt. His body was held for three days at the Egyptian border at Rafah that connects Egypt and the Gaza Strip before the family was allowed to bring it over and give the man a decent burial. In many countries it is normal to keep the body at a funeral home for a few days before the burial, but in our culture we feel that an early burial maintains the dignity of the deceased. However, occupation has no respect for human dignity. Under occupation, a border crossing can even become a funeral home. Thus it was that the body of Jamil had to wait for three days on the Egyptian side of the border, without any solemn music or a fancy casket.

I could not help but wonder: If it took three days for one dead man to be allowed to return to his hometown, how long will it take for the millions of Palestinian refugees scattered all over the world for decades to be allowed to return home?

The long years of military occupation and its harsh measures have offered continuous challenges, but also opportunities for reflection. We have tried to understand, to make sense out of all that was happening, and to find hope despite all the desperation. Easter time offers a particular occasion for reflection. Easter in the Holy Land has a very special meaning for us as both Palestinians and as Christians. The maximum extent of sacrifice is realized in the crucifixion of our Lord Jesus Christ for our redemption. And the maximum possibility of hope is derived from the empty tomb. Al Masseeh Qam. Haqqan Qam! That is how we greet each other on Easter Sunday. Christ has risen; He has risen indeed.

Perhaps that is why I, as a Christian, and so many other Christian Palestinians, relate so closely to Easter. Our young people continue to sacrifice their lives so that we can regain our freedom and our rights. Yet at the same time, with every young victim fallen, we try not to despair. We continue to hope that justice and peace will eventually prevail.

Despite all the stress of the *Intifada*, I was determined to celebrate the day before Easter Sunday, Holy Saturday, when the light appears from the empty tomb at the Church of the Holy Sepulcher[10]. But there was no way we could enter the Old City. My six-year-old grandson kept complaining about the many checkpoints as we tried to get through one of the Gates of Jerusalem. "We just want to attend Holy Saturday celebrations, so why don't they allow us in?" The Israeli military has a clichéd answer, always. The checkpoints are there for "security" reasons, and nobody dares question that. That day, the military seemed to be greater in number than the worshippers. That is probably what it was like under the Roman occupation during the days of Christ, which is another reason we relate so closely to Easter. How could I truly pray or meditate amid such surroundings? In a way, I was relieved that we could not enter the church, although I wanted so badly to light a candle of thanksgiving for the safety of our cousin Amin and his wife Samira, whose home had been shelled in Ramallah the week before. They were saved by a miracle, but had to move to their son's home for fear of another attack on their area. They eventually left the country completely.

All of this brought memories of another Holy Saturday at the church of the Holy Sepulcher before 1967. My uncle Wadie, my mother's brother, had arrived from Beirut, where he and his family had rebuilt their lives after the catastrophe of 1948. We all accompanied him to the special service of Holy Saturday. How different that Holy Saturday was! All those beautiful memories were marred by this brutal military occupation. Holy Saturday has taken on even more significance to me now, as it was on Holy Saturday, April 10, 2004, that my husband passed away. Holy Saturday has become a personal celebration as I remember a full life with a loving husband, father, and grandfather.

On the way back home on that Saturday morning, after our thwarted efforts to enter the church of the Holy Sepulcher, I started

---

10 This is a ritual of the Orthodox Church whereby it is believed that the light comes out of the tomb of Jesus Christ at the Holy Sepulcher on Easter Saturday. The Orthodox Patriarch passes the flame out to the community, and it is passed on to different areas of the country. Some of the faithful even carry the flame abroad in lanterns.

thinking of Elias Samaan Eid, a Christian Palestinian policeman who had been killed two days earlier, during Holy Week. The Israeli army had attacked the Khan Younis refugee camp in the Gaza Strip on April 12, 2001. The devastation caused by that attack left most of the camp residents homeless. Elias tried to protect the defenseless population of the camp, and he will always be remembered for his bravery. In sacrificing his life for the community, Elias not only emphasized the unity and common destiny of both Christian and Muslim Palestinians, but became a symbol as well of Christ's compassion for all people alike. How much hope can Elias's wife and five children have, now that he is gone?

But then, all the measures of the Israeli occupation forces do eventually lead to desperation. That is why the biggest challenge for parents, teachers and civil society volunteers has been to help people not to despair and to maintain their hope. Desperation can be very contagious. Very often it feels like one is swimming against the tide, as restrictive measures get tighter and new regulations force many to leave the country.

As the days went by, the situation worsened. For the first time since the beginning of the second *Intifada* I felt scared. Tears flowed as I remembered the pertinent words of the gospel according to Mark: "My soul is overwhelmed with sorrow to the point of death" (Mark 14:34).

Some of the Palestinian factions started resorting to suicide attacks to resist the occupation. Although it was very sad and very tragic, such actions were not completely unexpected. How docile can a nation remain when it has been dispossessed and deprived of its rights for over half a century? How restrained can people be when they have been oppressed under a brutal military occupation? Palestinians have been humiliated, dehumanized, deprived of their identity and their dignity, jailed, deported, and assassinated. They have had their lands confiscated, their homes demolished, and their orchards and groves completely razed. Did anybody really expect them to succumb peacefully to all these atrocities, and to thank the Israelis for the blessings of the occupation? Yet Israel retaliates mercilessly to the action of one desperate suicide bomber, using American supplied F16 bombers against a defenseless population. Were this to be done by any other military force than Israel, the whole world would be up in arms calling for a war crimes tribunal. I believe the US and Israel will eventually pay a heavy price for their policies.

Of course, without the support of the US administration the occupation could not have been maintained for such a long time. That is why, when the American SS Cole was attacked in the Gulf in October 2000, an American friend of mine commented that she was surprised that not more American interests in the Middle East were attacked. Truly, it is surprising.

Meanwhile, so many of our young people seem to think that the U.S. is Utopia, and that the dream of a better future lies there. Unfortunately, however, the genuine and friendly people who reflect that Utopia are not the same people who are abusing their power and forging the government's policy on Capitol Hill.

As Palestinians we have already paid our share of the bill for the sake of peace. Despite the injustice of the partition scheme of 1947 and the creation of the state of Israel on the ruins of Palestine, the PLO leadership made the historic concession to recognize the state of Israel, and to establish the Palestinian state alongside the state of Israel on territories occupied in 1967 – territories that comprise only 22% of historic Palestine. Many of us still think that one secular democratic state in all of historic Palestine would be the ideal solution to the conflict.

Despite that compromise, peace on 22% of historic Palestine has never been realized, and has in fact become a mirage. As Charley Reese stated in his column in the Orlando Sentinel on May 8, 2001, "The peace process is dead." Jeff Halper of ICHAD, the Israeli Committee Against House demolition, confirmed this as well in an essay titled, "Is the Two State Solution Dead?" (Link magazine, April-June 2012). And in his book, *The General's Son: Journey of an Israeli in Palestine*, Miko Peled confirms the impossibility of the two state solution. However, Uri Avnery, founder of the Gush Shalom peace movement, has not given up on the two state solution, and still thinks it is both possible and necessary.

When I think of the time that was wasted and the lives that were lost, Palestinians as well as Israelis, I cannot stop envisioning what life might be like in peaceful times. Will we ever be privileged to experience such a life? Will the younger generation, who has been exposed to so much brutality, ever be able to overcome their experiences? I certainly hope so. I know it took my nephew Bassem some time to get over the trauma of losing his friend on the football field in El-Bireh next to Ramallah. He and a score of young players were enjoying a game one afternoon in late July 2001 when an Israeli army jeep zoomed around the football field and opened fire, killing Nasser, the fellow next to Bassem. In a moment, the simple freedom of a football game was cut short by this ferocious killing.

On July 8, 2001, the first Sunday after the incident on the soccer field, I went to church to give thanks and light a candle for the safety of Bassem. I found it difficult to come to terms with my faith. "Until when, Dear Lord, until when?" I prayed, recognizing that the victim of that incident could have easily been my own nephew.

It was shortly after that incident, towards the end of August, when the Israeli army invaded Beit Jala, the town that had lost so much of its land to the settlement of Gilo. The first news that came out of the area was about the fifteen children from the Lutheran school who were taken hostage to serve as human shields for the protection of the Israeli Military Forces. It was ironic that the strongest military power in the Middle East needed children to protect them! Next we heard from Hanna Hallak, the cousin of my husband, that the house of his sister Hilda, had been occupied by the army. As if the occupation of the entire country was not enough, the army had to invade people's privacy and occupy their very homes.

Hilda's husband, Edmund Shihadeh, the Director of the Palestinian Rehabilitation Centre in Beit Jala, was out of town when this occupation took place. Hilda and her son were forced to stay downstairs with their neighbors, all in one room. Hilda was allowed to make a brief telephone call to her brother to let him know that she was all right. Another house was taken over as well, and a watch post was put on the roof. With the escalation of events, we kept wondering who would be the next victim.

Eventually Yousef and I visited Beit Jala. The many obstacles and detours we faced reminded us how long it had been since we had last been there. We finally discovered roundabout roads that led us to Hilda and Edmund's home, and heard first hand of their horrible experience. They took us for a tour of the town to see the damage from the Israeli shelling. No wonder people feel so insecure that they are willing to pack up and leave their homes! But that is exactly what the Israeli government wants them to do. And then, of course, the Israeli military forces claim that they shell these towns because their "security" is threatened. Once again, in the name of "security" all atrocities are justified.

In solidarity with the people of the areas of Bethlehem and Beit Jala after their ordeal, a convoy including clergy, lay people and representatives of organizations drove into Bethlehem on October 23, 2001. I was part of that convoy, and it was a very moving experience for me. The event was widely covered by the press, so the Israeli tanks were nowhere to be seen as we entered Bethlehem and gathered in Manger Square. Many of the local people also joined us there, grateful that this act of solidarity gave them the opportunity to get out of their homes for a fresh breath of air and a short period of freedom.

As soon as all those religious personalities with their colorful regalia, and the cameras accompanying them, left the Manger Square, the Israeli tanks started shooting again. In the meantime, we had all—Christians of all denominations, as well as Muslims—gathered at St. Catherine's Church. When the Muslim cleric joined the Christian clergy in the processional into the church, and later at the altar, the applause was endless. He gave a message of peace and solidarity that the people responded to with yet more warm applause.

One could feel how in need the Palestinian population was of this Christian-Muslim solidarity, especially in this area where Israel had been trying to drive a wedge between Christians and Muslims[11].

We then proceeded to the Latin Patriarchate Seminary in Beit Jala to offer condolences to the bereaved families who had lost children during the recent clashes, and to express our solidarity with the community that had been terrorized by the Israeli Military for the second time in less than three months. Fr. Raed Abusahlia, the Chancellor of the Latin Patriarchate of Jerusalem at that time, was commended on his efforts to make that day especially meaningful for the people of the Bethlehem region. The fear of the people and the devastation was very palpable. We continued to pray and hope that they would be spared further suffering and killings.

Soon after the Bethlehem solidarity visit, three Episcopalian Bishops, Roy F. Cederholm Jr., Barbara C. Harris, and M. Thomas Shaw, demonstrated in front of the Israeli Consulate in Boston to protest the harsh measures being imposed in the Occupied Territories. We were sure that those Bishops were not going to be spared pressure and harassment as they translated their faith into action. How I recalled my father's words: "Had there been enough courageous Christian leaders raising their voices against the grave injustice at the time of the *Nakba* in 1948, the situation would have never deteriorated to that extent." Perhaps the Palestine Kairos document, "A Moment of Truth," issued by local Palestinians, clergy and lay men and women, will help the church and Christians abroad understand what this brutal occupation, and the lack of a solution to the problem, is doing to the whole region and to its people.

Western Christian leaders continue to be concerned about the emigration of Christians from the Holy Land. Conferences, seminars and meetings are held to address the seriousness of the issue, and

---

11 The US Commission on International Religious Freedom reported in 2007 that "according to both Christian and Muslim Palestinians, Israel was attempting to drive a wedge between the two communities by exaggerating reports of religious tension between them." http://www.refworld.org/publisher, Minority Rights Group International, PSE,49749cd12,0.html

studies are made in an attempt to analyze and understand it. In reality, however, no studies are necessary: the root cause of all this is the Israeli military occupation, an occupation that is suffocating every aspect of the lives of the Palestinians, both Christians and Muslims. The Bethlehem area, which seems to be the concern of so many Christians abroad, has lost most of its land to Israeli settlements, and has been isolated from Jerusalem by the Wall that snakes through the area. As indigenous Christians of the land from which the message of Christianity was sent to the whole world, we appreciate that concern; but, without action, like faith without deeds, it is dead (James 2:14). With regard to the occupation and its brutal measures that deprive people of their right of residency and their right of return, the prophetic voice of the church leadership needs to be raised repeatedly. And it needs to be translated into action that will eventually bring about the end of occupation.

It remains to be said that due to the occupation, Christians as well as Muslims have been leaving the country. The mosaic of Palestinian society is becoming increasingly less diverse, as more Christians emigrate. Of course, this is good news for Israel, so that it can turn the struggle into a Muslim-Jewish struggle. In such a struggle, the Jews would gain even more sympathy due to the Judeo-Christian tradition and the Jewish history in Europe. However, the Christians in Palestine are the oldest Christian community in the world. Although they have long been small in number, they have managed to survive and to assert their presence, raise their voice, and contribute to the development of their communities as committed active leaders, educators, artists, musicians, writers and volunteers, as well as through the church-related schools, organizations, hospitals, and other centers that have always served not just the Christian community but the whole Palestinian community.

Our Daily Life

On July 31, 2001, I wrote to a Swedish friend describing our daily life.

"Although we are trying very hard to lead a normal life, you can imagine how difficult this is when everything around us is so abnormal. It is not easy for you, as a young person and in a country like Sweden, to envisage what occupation means. It does not only mean the deprivation of a nation's freedom, but also the deprivation of one's personal freedom.

Since 1964, my husband, Yousef, and I have been living in Beit Hanina, a Palestinian suburb north of Jerusalem. We are located exactly midway between Jerusalem to the south, and Ramallah to the north. My sister lives in Ramallah, and my brother lives further north in the university town of Birzeit. Ever since the second Intifada and the closure of the areas, visiting with my sister and brother has become almost a burden. Normally the drive up to Ramallah takes 10-15 minutes and another 10 minutes to Birzeit. Now sometimes it takes hours to get there; that is, if one gets there. Some days it goes very smoothly, but you can never plan and never know what may happen. Very often my brother gets out of Birzeit, and on the way back he finds the road completely blocked. So I avoid travelling to Ramallah as much as possible.

From my home to Jerusalem there is no checkpoint, so I can continue with my voluntary work at the YWCA, at Rawdat El-Zuhur School, and at Sabeel Liberation Theology Centre without too many complications. But the work is very often disrupted because many members or staff cannot access the workplace regularly. Maybe I am more fortunate than others, particularly as both my children live in the same neighborhood. But the greatest daily worry for us is the grandchildren's commute to school. They all go to the Friends Quaker school in Ramallah. My daughter has two boys and a girl, and my son has two girls[12], but the younger one is still one year old. Their parents do not drive them to school because they cannot reach their work in time if they waste hours on the kids transport before returning to their work in Jerusalem. So we have a taxi taking them back and forth every day. I try to help out by preparing a hot meal for the children when they get back from school. But their daily trip to Ramallah has drained me, just worrying about their safety. I can never relax until I get word from the taxi that they made it safely across the checkpoint.

Summer holidays offer such a relief, but in a month's time schools will open and the problem has not been resolved, so we shall go back to the daily worry. How very often we panicked and asked some friends to pick up the children when the Israelis shelled Ramallah. We did not even contemplate sending them to a camp this summer, so as not to worry about their safety. Along with some of the cousins who live in the neighborhood, we planned a day camp for them in the basement of their apartment building, and Peter, the grandson of my father's cousin, volunteered to run the camp. He had enough experience, as he was practically brought up in the YMCA; his father Kamil and grandfather Labib before him were both directors of the YMCA of East Jerusalem.

Luckily my husband retired shortly before the Intifada and closed his office in Ramallah, so he is around to help with the grandchildren. He also continues to serve on the boards of some local organizations and heads a Housing Society, which has an office very close to our

---

12 Since I wrote that letter, my son had two boys.

Samia with Salwa Zananiri, Principal of Rawdat El-Zuhur

neighborhood. But compared to the people in Gaza, Hebron, and the northern towns of the Palestinian Territories we are in heaven. Israel is doing everything possible to make life absolutely intolerable for the Palestinian population.

Water sources are another worry for everyone in the area. Thanks to my husband, who had some vision when we built our house, we have two cisterns. Otherwise we would not have water. The country as a whole suffers from shortage of water, but it is frustrating to see the Israeli settlements flooded with green lawns and swimming pools, while we hardly have water for drinking and for bathing. I remember how much I enjoyed taking showers when I was in Sweden; I knew I was not depriving anybody from their essential quota of water. I hope you will always be grateful for what you have and which many young people take for granted, never realizing how precious freedom, democracy and water are."

Sabeel Liberation Theology Centre was the last organization that I got involved with in my long years of volunteer work. Ever since I got married in 1960 and started a family, I opted for volunteer work,

At the Sabeel International Conference in Jerusalem

With Doris after the World YWCA Council in Singapore

so that I could set my own hours. As early as 1961 I got involved with the YWCA, which gave me great opportunities to develop and get involved in women's empowerment and global issues, especially through the many World YWCA Council meetings that I attended. Later I started helping my aunt Lizzy Nasir, a social worker who had started a home for destitute girls begging on the streets. I carried on her legacy after the she retired in 1986, when the home had started to develop as a school. For seventeen years I worked closely with its principal, Salwa Zananiri, who had trained under my aunt. Salwa has kept the place a true haven for Palestinian children from Jerusalem and its suburbs, and has provided the same caring spirit and moral values as my aunt established. Now the school is run by a younger team, and is still providing quality education for children, with the same loving spirit and values. As the YWCA and Rawdat El-Zuhur were both affiliated to the Palestinian non-governmental organization (PNGO), there was a lot of work to be done on the national level, helping prisoners and visiting the injured in hospitals. I also had the privilege of representing PNGO twice at UN forums in New York and Athens.

In 1989 I was invited by Rev. Naim Ateek, who was the pastor of the Anglican Church in Jerusalem, to join a group of clergy, lay men and women as founding members of a Palestinian liberation theology movement. He had written a book, *Justice and Only Justice*, which was the basis for the movement. In March 1990 we held our first international conference to assess the need for this new concept. International liberation theologians attended, and we succeeded beyond our expectations. The local community responded very positively. We started our work out of the office of Rev. Ateek, using the church hall for meetings, and were then given two rooms, after which we moved to independent premises. We registered the movement under the name of Sabeel Ecumenical Liberation Theology Centre. The work started with one volunteer, but now the centre engages a number of staff for a variety of programs. Sabeel has a branch in Nazareth, and has international friends of Sabeel in the UK, North America, Europe, the Oceania region and elsewhere. My welcoming address at the 1st International Conference of Sabeel, "*Faith and the Intifada*", which appears in Appendix VII, was published as the forward for the proceedings of the conference. Since then the centre has held eight international conferences, with an average of one conference each two to three years. International adult conferences have been held annually for the last seven years.

In summer 2012, the founding members as well as members of the first board stepped down and made room for the election of a younger team to assist Rev. Ateek in this vital ministry. Ever since I joined Sabeel, I began to relate to many biblical verses in the context of our situation. One of my favorites has been John 8:32: "You shall know the truth and the truth shall set you free." In fact, this verse was written on the archway of the hall of the first premises that we rented for the Sabeel offices in the Sheikh Jarrah quarter, before we moved to the present premises in Shufa'at. One of the major programs that Sabeel runs is speaking to groups. Hearing our story, those people really "get stuck with the truth." I can vouch that Rev. Ateek, along with Cedar, Jean, Nora, Omar and others have made more of an impact than many of our UN representatives and ministers of information. Hopefully the truth will eventually set the American Congress free. It seems that while the Palestinians are physically occupied by Israel, the majority of the American Congress is mentally and psychologically occupied by Israel, since at every Palestinian initiative there is always a threat that Congress will cut aid to the Palestinians.

At the World Conference on Racism in Durban, South Africa, in September 2001, Zionism was discussed clearly and critically. For a long time both Israel and the US have been held hostage to the myths about Israel's creations: that Israel was "a land without people for a people without a land," and "the only democracy in the Middle East." In reality, Israel was established on the ethnic cleansing of the indigenous people of the land, while justifying all its violations of human rights in the name of security. At Durban, the truth was exposed. But this exposure proved too much for Israel and the US, to cope with. Pulling out of the conference was the easiest exit. However, not facing the issue does not mean it is going to disappear. In the meantime, life under occupation was getting more and more difficult. Birzeit, my home-town, was not easily accessible any more. In fact, with the increasing number of checkpoints and curfews imposed, traveling to Birzeit has become a nightmare. But on November 9, 2001, I was determined to make that trip, come rain or sunshine, checkpoints or barricades.

The last time I had been there was in mid July for the graduation ceremony at Birzeit University. This time it was quite different. Making the trip required a lot of planning. Driving through the Qalandia checkpoint would take forever. So I hired a taxi to drop me off at that point, and then I walked across and picked up a taxi to the Surda checkpoint, named after the little town of Surda on the way between Ramallah and Birzeit. The only cars that could drive through the checkpoint were the yellow taxis, and they would take forever also, because the army takes its sweet time checking every car. So once again I did the crossing on foot. It was lovely to see my brother Hanna on the other side waiting for me. Hanna could not resist a detour to the university campus before we reached the family home, where Tania had fresh chilled lemonade ready for us. He had put a huge amount of effort into fund raising for the various buildings, and he wanted to show me the new Physical Education Building, which was almost finished, and some of the new roads built to facilitate driving around the campus.

What a joy it was to be in Birzeit again and to visit with the family, especially with my nephew, Ramzi, the young physician. On this visit, for the first time I was carrying a cellular phone; my daughter Dina had talked me into entering the era of technology. It helps under these peculiar circumstances to feel that you can get

Yousef and Samia enjoying retirement

in touch with the family if something goes wrong; and in Palestine there's no end to what can go wrong. Ramzi is Hanna and Tania's son; he had come from the States almost a month ago and had been scheduled to travel back before we could see him. Birzeit was practically under siege during that period; the Israeli Military Forces had entered into the northern part of Ramallah and imposed a curfew. So Ramzi could not travel. But there was a positive side to the situation: for Hanna, who always worries about his health, it was a relief to have a doctor in the house.

We had a relaxing and enjoyable visit, but it was too short. I had set off to Birzeit late, because we had a breakfast at Rawdat El-Zuhur to launch the 50th anniversary calendar. I really wanted to visit friends and family in Birzeit, but I had to be in Ramallah at 4:30 for an executive meeting of Sabeel. It is not always easy to travel across the checkpoint, so we usually try to combine many meetings into those precious visits. We met at Cedar Duaybis' home, where Jean Zaru and Rev. Ateek joined us. Cedar was still living in Ramallah, where her husband had been posted as pastor of St. Andrews Anglican Church in 1986. Sadly, her husband had passed away in 1990, shortly after he had retired. All went well with our visit until Rev. Ateek and I crossed the Qalandia checkpoint on the way back and found there were no cars on the other side to take us back to Jerusalem. We called his wife Maha to come and meet us, and in the meantime we started walking. I must admit it would have been good exercise, if only the road had not been so dusty, bumpy and stinky, with an awful smell from open sewage and from the piles of garbage rotting all around. Maha was delayed on the checkpoint out of Jerusalem, but finally reached us after we had walked for more than half a kilometer. Then, of course, we got stuck in the traffic, with further delay on the checkpoint going into Jerusalem. We eventually made it home, and it was one of those times that I was grateful there was water in the tap: a good hot shower from top to toe helped me cleanse the agony and dust of the day.

Soon after that trip it became increasingly impossible to reach Surda by car, much less Birzeit. The cars would stop in the middle of the first road out of Ramallah, known to many people in the area as Nazlelt el-Sheikh Yousef. People had to walk all the way down to where the garbage dump was, which has now turned into a road leading to a settlement, and then back uphill to catch the cars on the other side. The cart and mule became a popular means of transportation for the elderly and for many who could not make that stretch daily. As in every calamity there are always people who benefit, and the cart and mule turned into a new business. That is, until the morning of July 27, 2003, when my brother called cheerfully to let me know that the road was finally open to regular transportation all the way from Ramallah to Birzeit and vice versa. My first reaction was, the mules are out of a job!

Announcements regarding easing restrictions had failed to materialize in the past, however, we waited to see whether things would improve or not. Although I felt skeptical about it, I hoped it would be a permanent measure.

For Hanna, as President of the University, that roadblock had been his nightmare, a nightmare shared by thousands of students and faculty over the past year. One must raise a hat to all of them for their determination to trudge forward in spite of the hardships of their daily Via Dolorosa. Up the hills and down the vales, around piles of dirt, and with the help of mules and carriages, they made their way, and graduation did take place at the beginning of the month. In addition, Hanna's daughter and first grandchild had just arrived from the States, so one wonderful thing about the lifted restrictions was that the family could now drive through Surda and be together.

The latest story that one of my grandchildren brought home the other day is that the Palestinians are guaranteed to go straight to heaven. Do you know why? Because by now they know all the by-pass roads!

The happy news for the people of Birzeit and the surrounding villages was a disaster for the mules and their owners. However, since there are still hundreds of roadblocks in the territories, I assume they can pick up their business somewhere else. Normally there would have been plenty of business for them plowing olive groves. But under occupation even those groves have become inaccessible or lost, as the Israeli settlers and military deny people access to their groves, or simply confiscate them for "security reasons." The monstrous Wall is literally swallowing thousands of acres of farming land. Every day there is another announcement about land confiscations: 400 dunoms here, another 500 dunoms there[13]. It is a daily broadcast. Only the quantities and locations change, as the confiscations continue all the way from the neighborhoods of Jerusalem and Bethlehem to the heart of the West Bank, identified according to the Oslo Accords as area C[14].

As Christmas approached that year, I knew the holiday season would have a different meaning after so much devastation and loss of lives during the preceding year. Too much lamenting supersedes the joy of the occasion, yet no amount of lamenting will bring back dear ones or build demolished homes. In the US as well, the memory of September 11, 2001 was bound to mar the Christmas celebrations. But I was hoping for the sake of my American and British friends that their young people would be home for Christmas after the futile Gulf War. Despite the depressing mood and the feeling of hopelessness encompassing the whole region, we felt that there was more need than ever to cheer up the children of Rawdat El-Zuhur school before the holidays. We could not have chosen a better Santa Claus for the children than my nephew Marwan. He charmed the

---

13 One dunom =1000sq.m

14 The Oslo Accord II created three temporary distinct administrative divisions in the West Bank until a final status accord would be established: Areas A, B and C. Area A is under full civil and security control by the Palestinian Authority, Area B is under Palestinian civil control and joint Israeli-Palestinian security control, and Area C is under full Israeli civil and security control, except over Palestinian civilians.

children and showered them with bags of gifts. It was a pleasure to see how happy the children were. After all, that is what this season is all about: joy, peace, and love.

As I started sending greetings to friends and family abroad, my greetings crumbled under the distress of what I narrated. I could not help but think of the euphoria of 1993, when the Israeli army tanks were leaving the Palestinian Territories after Oslo and the youth showered the tanks with roses. Despite its flaws, I do not think anybody envisaged that the peace process would deteriorate to this extent. Those same tanks are now back in the Palestinian Territories, storming, devastating, and terrorizing the population.

The people of Ramallah are scared to death that hell will truly break loose. The military barged into my sister Rima's house, looking for arms. My friend Cedar, who lives so close to Headquarters of Mr. Arafat, fled her house with her daughter and granddaughter to stay in a safer place. They do not know whether their home was rampaged or not. But at this point it is irrelevant: what matters is their safety. Thank heavens, the telephone where they are staying in the church compound is still functioning, but they have no electricity. An American friend of theirs was on the telephone when the soldiers entered her house. They threatened to kill her cat if she stayed on the phone and said anything. Eventually they cut the telephone line, devoured her fruit plate and left. When eventually things calmed down, Cedar found out that her home had been brutally ransacked. There wasn't one thing in its place. It took her a long while to be able to overcome the shock of seeing her home in that condition, and to remove the filth that those soldiers left behind. In the meantime, her granddaughter Juman, who, along with her mother, lived with Cedar, was petrified after that ugly experience and especially by the heavy shelling that took place close to their home. The ten year old was hanging on to her mother day and night in order to feel safe. She expressed her fear in a very unusual way: she said, "Khayfeh min el-Khouf" (I am afraid of fear). What memories have they left for those children to live with?

The day after Easter, on April 1, 2002, the Israeli army invaded the Jenin Refugee Camp as part of Operation Defensive Shield, sealing the area off for eleven days. While the army continued to rampage the whole area, forbidding entrance to any reporters or international inspectors, there were rumors of a massacre. The United Nations inquiry team was not allowed to investigate. When people eventually started coming out of the camp, Jenin seemed to be a restaging of the nightmare of the 1948 trauma.

Jenin 2002 was 1948 remembered. I was in my early teens at boarding school in Birzeit when the first stream of people from Ramleh and Lydda started arriving into town. They had been driven out at gunpoint by the Zionist underground forces and had been walking for miles. En route they had lost dear ones, and as they were searched on their way out, they had been robbed of a lot of their money and jewelry. According to eyeWitnesses, the Israelis took earlobes along with the earrings, fingers with the rings, and hands and even arms with their bracelets.

Birzeit and Ramallah were the first two towns where some of these people found refuge. I can still remember how we went out to the street to invite them in for a meal after that horrific experience and their tedious journey on foot. Aunt Nabiha ordered the kitchen staff to bring out whatever food supplies were available in the storeroom to prepare a meal for those refugees. Some were in a complete daze; others were so relieved to find some food and water. I specifically remember one woman who went on and on, talking incoherently. Somebody told us that she might have sunstroke and be delirious. The sight of those people lying around in the school hall, in the churches, and under the olive trees has haunted me for decades; the images are still vivid after fifty-four years.

The residents of the Jenin camp—themselves victims of the *Nakba*—are now reliving the 1948 trauma once again. Those who were babies or young teenagers at that time have had no other home but this camp. It is where they have been brought up, gone to school, worshipped, got married, and settled down. It is where their parents and grandparents were buried as they waited relentlessly for their right of return to be realized. Once again the month of April, which Witnessed the Deir Yassin Massacre in 1948, has been Witness to another tragedy for the refugee population of the Jenin camp. The unknown is what makes this tragedy so horrific, as reports and stories keep trickling out of a possible massacre taking place inside.

But Israel claims it has nothing to hide, and that is why it did not allow any human rights activists, reporters, or medical teams to enter at the time of the incursion. In fact, Israel, which has been defying all United Nations resolutions, has even succeeded this time to make a mockery out of the United Nations as it contemplated sending a fact-finding mission. So much for that mission.

Nonetheless, credible voices like Terje Roed-Larsen were heard describing the scene as "horrific beyond belief' and that it was' "morally repugnant to bar medical and humanitarian aid for eleven days."

Almost at the same time, and still as part of Operation Defensive Shield, Israeli Forces invaded Bethlehem on April 2, 2002, reoccupying the town they had withdrawn from, along with other major Palestinian towns, at the beginning of the Peace Process. Palestinian security forces and others took refuge in the church of the Nativity, which remained under siege until May 10. Two hundred Palestinians took refuge in the Church of the Nativity while the Israeli Forces sent threatening messages that they would storm the Church if those hiding inside did not go out. The Governor of Bethlehem was one of the people inside the church, along with many other civilians who happened to be in the wrong place at the wrong time. One of them was Garo, a Jerusalem photographer who was accompanying some reporters. The Palestinian policemen who took refuge in the church handed their arms to the priests before entering the church the day Bethlehem was reoccupied. When the Israeli Forces threw a bomb, which started a fire in the church, a Palestinian policeman ran out to extinguish the fire and was shot dead by an Israeli sniper.

The situation continued to be incredibly tense. The community was very appreciative of the church authorities, in particular of the Latin Patriarch, for providing a haven for the people from the brutality of the Israeli Military. All the churches were praying for peace. The Franciscan brothers inside the church, within their limited means, were trying their best to provide comfort to the people as the days of siege went on. Maybe that incident helped to remove the wedge that Israel is continuously driving between Muslims and Christians. The Church of the Nativity, which has survived so many invasions and wars, even the brutality of the Persians, was now under threat of being stormed. I kept wondering whether the voice of the Christian World would be loud enough to put an end to all this brutality, inhumanity and injustice.

Eventually, after 39 days, an agreement was reached to lift the siege. Under the terms of the agreement, those Palestinians wanted by the Israeli forces would be deported either to Gaza or to Europe. Since the Israeli army had already withdrawn from the Palestinian Territories in 1995, in compliance with the Oslo Accords, there was no justification for them to be in Bethlehem in the first place. So the agreement to deport the hostages to Gaza or to Europe was unfair and unjustified. But that is what happened. The Oslo Accords never guaranteed security to the Palestinians, or an end to Israeli incursions into the Palestinian Territories. Those who were deported are still struggling to come back.

Onslaught on Jerusalem

Evictions

On Sunday, August 2, 2009, life for the Hanoun and Ghawi families was turned upside down. Under the pretext that their family residences in Jerusalem had been Jewish property before 1948, the Israeli Forces evicted them from their homes in the Sheikh Jarrah quarter, a Palestinian neighborhood, and Jewish settlers immediately occupied the houses. Although all of our community rallied in solidarity, we could do nothing more than watch as the helpless parents tried to comfort their traumatized children.

I used to pass by the Hanoun house regularly on my way to the YWCA, which was almost like a second home for me. We were working hard to provide programs for the Jerusalem community to help people cope with the new reality of occupation. Given the memories of 1948 evictions and the ensuing scattering of the Palestinians all over the world, almost every Palestinian can relate to the brutality of an eviction. The eviction of the Hanoun and Ghawi families disturbed me so much that I could not get myself to go to church; I felt too angry. This time I felt like screaming, not just pleading, "How Long, O Lord, How Long?"

Protest in front of the Hanoun house in Sheikh Jarrah

Once again Israel had challenged the whole world with impunity. Both the US administration, and the United Nations, stood impotent, unable to take action against Israel for these violations of human rights and international law. The irony is that the area from which those families were evicted is to go to a settlement called "Shimon Ha Tzaddik" (Simon the pious). Can the eviction of people be considered an act of piety? To suggest so is just as ironic as building a "Museum of Tolerance" on the remains of the Muslim cemetery in the Mamilla area in Jerusalem, as Israel announced in 2011 it would do. Neither the living nor the dead can rest in peace under a military occupation.

Almost a year earlier, on November 9, 2008, the Al-Kurd family was also evicted from their home in the same neighborhood of Sheikh Jarrah, after a seven-year dispute with settlers who had occupied half of their house. That house was part of a housing project built by the Jordanian government and UNWRA for Palestinian refugees in 1956. Israel, however, claimed that it was Jewish property before 1948. Should that be the justification behind the eviction, it would be logical that Palestinians now living in East Jerusalem should claim their stolen property in West Jerusalem. After all, since Israel declares that Jerusalem is one united city, its residents should have the same rights in both parts of the city. But the Israeli logic that prevails is, "What's mine is mine, and what's yours is mine."

In 2010 Haaretz, the Israeli English language newspaper, published an interview with Claudette Ayyoub Habesch, a Palestinian woman living in East Jerusalem, in which Habesch discussed her intention to raise a case against the Israeli government to claim her family's property in West Jerusalem[15]. Under the circumstances, she knows very well she cannot evict anybody, but she is demanding that her right be recognized. The case is one more example of the non-violent resistance that the Palestinians have been pursuing.

As far back as 2000, and perhaps even earlier, the late Faisal Husseini had called on all the Jerusalemites who had property in West Jerusalem to document their title deeds and submit them to the Arab Studies Society at the Orient House. He had plans to build a legal case based on the rights of those who had fled or who were evicted from their homes in 1948. Sadly, the project did not materialize. Faisal passed away, and on August 10, 2001, the occupation forces finally succeeded in shutting down the Orient House by military order. During his lifetime, Faisal had challenged every closure order, and had been able to keep the Orient House open. Despite all the protests, the closure order has been renewed every year.

Faisal's vision for Jerusalem was for Palestinians to develop and run the different service sectors. He got the European Union to support a Multi-Sector Review, and I had the privilege of serving on the committee for the education sector. The youth of Jerusalem were one of our main concerns, as we felt that the occupation was corrupting them morally. In Arabic, the word Ihtilal, meaning occupation, is ironically very similar to the word Inhilal, meaning moral corruption. The youth, whom we considered to be the hope for the future, had as children during the first *Intifada* been in the forefront resisting the occupation. But now they seemed to have become a cause of worry for the whole community. It only took a

---

15 *Haaretz*, July 23, 2010, weekend edition.

short tour through the streets of Jerusalem to observe the pathetic situation of the youth, clustered lethargically in the streets or roaming about recklessly with their noisy cars. The number of drug addicts and school dropouts has been on the rise, with devastating results. Within this context, it has become imperative that the building of Jerusalem as the capital of the future independent Palestinian state must first and foremost be based on the character-building of Palestinian citizens. Unfortunately, after more than a decade the youth remain at a loss. In some areas, the situation has become practically hopeless. But the Jerusalem organizations have not given up; they are working with the youth through various cultural activities and sports in an effort to salvage an entire generation.

Faisal Husseini Ibrahim Abu-Lughod and Edward Said

When Faisal Husseini died, the whole country grieved his loss. I still remember that sad day. It was May 31, 2001, the last day of school at Rawdat El-Zuhur. One of the teachers said that she had heard that Faisal had passed away. I could not believe it. I simply had to rush to the Orient House and see for myself. It was true; he had passed away in Kuwait while trying to mend relations between the PLO and Kuwait. His last mission was that of peace and reconciliation. June 1, 2001, the day of the funeral, was a day of sadness, a day of defiance, and a day of assertion for Arab Jerusalem. Faisal had been the living symbol of Jerusalem, the strong voice of the city that we rallied around and listened to. He had seemed the only reference point left for us in Jerusalem as we struggled under siege during that period after the "peace process" started. He was so humble; so full of hope and optimism. His death shook us to the core.

Just a week before his demise we had all been in Jaffa with Edward Said, eulogizing Professor Ibrahim Abu-Lughod who was, according to Edward, the leading Arab academic activist in North

America. Ibrahim had founded the Association of Arab American University Graduates. He was professor of political science at Northwestern University for 34 years before he resigned, becoming one of the first Palestinian academicians to return home and teach at Birzeit University. The loss was too much for us to take: Ibrahim and Faisal, two of our best, gone one after another.

And then, almost two years later, Edward Said was gone as well. With his passing in 2003, the world lost a great champion of humanity. And what a terrible time to lose him: during that crucial period we needed his vision and intellect more than ever. Most of all we needed his integrity; his courage in speaking out for truth and justice. We have an Arabic proverb: "If words are of silver, then silence is of gold." But this never applied to Edward. For him, silence meant weakness and capitulation. He spoke so strongly against Israeli military occupation and its colonial policies and oppressive measures. He was also critical of the US administration for its blind support of Israel, and for the double standards with which it dealt with Israel and the Palestinians. And he was just as critical of the PNA. He criticized the Oslo Accords, not because he was against peace but because he could not keep silent while so many concessions were being made at the expense of the inalienable rights of the Palestinians, including the right of return. I still recall the excitement we all felt at his first visit to Palestine, when he was awarded an honorary doctorate in Humanities from Birzeit University in 1993. I had not seen him since 1947, when I had met him as a young boy at the wedding of my cousin Huda to his cousin George. In 1998 he was invited to be the keynote speaker at the Sabeel International Conference, which was held at the auditorium of Bethlehem University. The auditorium could not cope with the number of people, including Palestinians from the pre-1948 area, who flooded in to hear him that evening. A large screen was set up to project his speech live to the audience in an adjacent hall. That gathering turned out to be a Palestinian tribute to Edward while he was still alive.

The demolishing of Abu Aishah house in Beit Hanina

Faisal's funeral was such as the city had never seen before. The road from Ramallah, where the helicopter bringing him from Jordan landed, was filled with mourners all the way to the Haram El-Sharif in Jerusalem. Cars with Palestinian flags defied all the checkpoints and entered Jerusalem. The city under siege, where such great efforts are made to prevent Palestinians from having access, could not keep Palestinians out that day. Faisal's funeral cortege went through the streets of Jerusalem. The Orient House, where Faisal had his office and which, like Faisal himself, had become the symbol of Arab Jerusalem, was filled with a large gathering of people who came to mourn him from as far as the Golan Heights. The Syrian flag bearers stood in front of the Druze Sheiks and notables, who formed a human chain, chanting words of grief for the great loss for Palestine and Jerusalem. The Israeli police, who normally made a presence at every gathering of solidarity Faisal had called for at the Orient House, were nowhere to be seen, even when the young men hung the Palestinian flag on top of the Court House and the Post Office buildings in the heart of Jerusalem.

Just as Faisal's death enabled the powerful manifestation of Arab Jerusalem, so did Professor Ibrahim Abu Lughod acquire his right of return to Jaffa through his burial in his hometown. His funeral cortege left from the Maqassed hospital in Jerusalem. Despite the closures and the restrictions on movement, Ibrahim's friends from the Occupied Territories joined Palestinians who had stayed in the devastated town of Jaffa and many other Palestinians from behind the Green Line. Together we formed a powerful presence, defying the reality of dispossession as the Palestinian flag hovered in the skies over Jaffa. Proudly, Palestinian men lifted Ibrahim's body, wrapped with a Palestinian flag, into the mosque for prayers. Ibrahim was laid to rest to the sound of the everlasting symphony of the sea he loved so much. Professor Abu-Lughod, an American Palestinian, returned to his homeland in 1991 to serve at Birzeit University. He taught political science and served as Vice President, and he also established the faculty of graduate studies. I will always cherish the memory of those days in Birzeit where I was volunteering when Professor Abu Lughud came back to Palestine. I was privileged to work with him, and no matter how tough the going was, he always made my day with his charming smile and everlasting optimism.

Faisal, who had almost the same pleasant disposition and optimism as Professor Abu-Lughod, was not only missed on the political scene; he was greatly missed on the popular level as well, for he had always been present at the various social, religious and cultural functions of our community. He was deeply committed to the welfare of Jerusalem and its people, and he paid heavily for that commitment through continuous harassment by the military occupation. We lost track of the number of times he was in jail or under house arrest. But he always managed to come out of it with dignity, and with a beautiful smile that never left his face. His presence always made a difference, in the context of defying the occupation. I still recall the peaceful candle light march in 1996 in the old city of Jerusalem, which Faisal and Rev. Ateek from Sabeel led. Along with many other Christian and Muslim leaders, they had first prayed at St. Anne's church to protest the opening of the tunnel under Al-Aqsa Mosque. Faisal also joined the Jerusalem community at the Tombs of the Kings for the opening of the Yabous Cultural Centre's first festival in 1996; this festival eventually became an annual function that brought life to the city.

Home Demolitions

On July 28, 2008, I sat down to write about the Jerusalem Festival at the Tombs of the Kings, but my mood changed completely when I heard news of the demolition of the five story building of Majed Abu Eisheh in Beit Hanina. A few months before, the Israeli authorities had issued a demolition order for the building, because the family did not have the correct license for as many floors as were built. The owners started the process of getting the license. In the meantime,

A view of Silwan the coveted neighborhood near Al-Aqsa Mosque

a lot of pressure was exerted to avert the demolition while the licensing was being processed. Unfortunately, the efforts were to no avail. The pattern has become all too familiar. The Israeli authorities warn people, but when pressure is at its highest they back off, only to return later on, when the community has relaxed and the world media is silent about the issue.

The Israeli authority is very careful that demolitions as well as evictions and even deportations always take place in the early hours of the morning, when there is nobody to Witness or stand in solidarity to prevent such illegal and immoral actions. Even the confiscation of the car of a friend, Laila, who was working at the French Consulate, took place after midnight in order to avoid any pressure or media involvement. Ever since the illegal annexation of East Jerusalem, all staff of consulates, church-related organizations and international NGO's have been exempt from paying taxes. But by 2004 Israel was already trying to revoke that privilege. While negotiations were still taking place, Laila was the victim and her new Nissan car was the target. The Israeli police confiscated the car after midnight. She needed that car badly, because she was taking care of her brother with Downs Syndrome; her brother always looked forward to a drive after Laila got home from work. One would think that Israel, the so called "civilized"country, the professed "only democracy" in the Middle East, would resort to more civilized methods of implementing illegal laws. Not that they had a right to Laila's car, but they could have easily picked it up from the French Consulate during working hours if need be.

The demolition of the Abu Aishah house was one in a long list of home demolitions. Although Israel claims that it demolishes homes because the owners do not have building permits, it never alludes to the fact that Israel makes it very difficult, and indeed often almost impossible, for Palestinians in Jerusalem to obtain building permits to develop their own property. I remember that it took us seven years to get a permit for building the second floor at Rawdat El-Zuhur. ICAHD (the Israeli Committee Against House Demolitions) challenges such Israeli actions, trying to stop demolitions and rebuilding demolished homes. Israeli forces demolished Beit-Arabiya, the ICAHD peace centre, for the fifth time on January 23, 2012, and during the autumn of 2012 it was demolished for the sixth time. However, there are Israeli peace activists who continue to protest against these illegal and inhuman policies and measures of their government. In fact, ever since the eviction of the families in Sheikh Jarrah took place, Israeli peace activists have been protesting weekly every Friday afternoon in the Sheikh Jarrah area.

On July 13, 2009, Israeli forces demolished two more homes in Silwan and Beit Hanina. Silwan is one of Jerusalem's southern neighborhoods, and is very close to Al-Aqsa Mosque. Israel has been coveting Silwan ever since it occupied the city in 1967, especially since it started excavation works under the whole neighborhood. In 2002, the municipality of Jerusalem decided to demolish 88 houses of Al-Bustan quarter in Silwan to build a garden. The residents of the neighborhood continue to protest, but already at the entrance of Silwan a sign has been put up with the name "David City." The Judaization of the area is ongoing despite all the protests of the residents and their supporters. A Youtube video has been circulating since the beginning of 2013, showing the Jewish Temple replacing the Al-Aqsa Mosque. It should not come as a great surprise that the excavations will eventually jeopardize the foundations of the Mosque. Palestine TV news reported almost on a daily basis during February 2013 on settlers storming the mosque; they reported that Israel is planning to build a structure adjacent to the Buraq wall.

Since the beginning of 2012, the media has been reporting daily on eviction orders, land confiscations, and demolition of homes in East Jerusalem and elsewhere in the West Bank. Early in February 2013, all the people of Beit Safafa, a southern suburb of Jerusalem, went out to protest the building of a highway in the midst of the town. The struggle to prevent the building of the Wall on the land of the Cremisan Monestry in Beit Jala is still ongoing.

According to Gush Shalom[16], the building of settlements in 2011 increased by 20%. And according to the report of OCHA, the UN Office for Coordination of Humanitarian Affairs, attacks by settlers against Palestinians at the end of 2011 were up 32 percent from 2010 and 144 percent from 2009. These include attacks against Palestinians that result in injury or death as well as attacks against Palestinian property. Up until August 7, 2012, OCHA reported that 26 settlers had received injuries as a result of violence by Palestinians, while 89 Palestinians had received injuries caused by settler violence.

---

16 Gush Shalom is an Israeli peace bloc that aims to influence Israeli public opinion and lead it towards peace and reconciliation with the Palestinian people.

These reports did not include the incident of August 16, 2012, when settlers burned a Palestinian taxi on the way to Arroub refugee camp near Hebron. Six adults and three children were seriously injured. It may have been this incident that triggered a very different kind of US response than usual: the US foreign secretary described the violence of settlers as terrorism. It seems the heat of August 2012 exacerbated the violence against the Palestinians, and this violence was not limited to settlers only. As of this writing, the latest incident was on August 17, 2012, when Jewish youth attacked three Palestinians in West Jerusalem and beat one of them nearly to death.

It is the same old story, repeated over and over again. Everybody protests: the Palestinian Authority says that such actions are illegal and that the building of Israeli settlements is an obstacle to the peace process. They even make bold statements to the effect that they will not allow this and that to happen. But sadly, they have no say in the matter, nor do they have power to revoke what has been done. Even Jordan which has a peace treaty with Israel and is supposed to be the Guardian of Al-Aqsa Mosque, has not taken any action to deter Israel from its onslaught on the area of Al-Aqsa Mosque. The US administration might ask, or even order, Israel not to demolish homes or build settlements. But that does not mean anything to Israel. Unfortunately, both the international community and even the Arab World keep appeasing Israel, while the UN has never had the guts to impose sanctions on Israel according to the same standards applied to other countries that do not abide by United Nations resolutions and international law.

Logic simply defies such double standards. It is greatly disappointing that all Mr. Ban Ki-moon, Secretary-General of the United Nations, can come up with is another empty statement to the effect that home demolitions are "contrary to international law" and "unhelpful" to efforts to restart peace negotiations. This is a familiar statement, one that has become meaningless to the Palestinians, and which does not even bother Israel any more. I wonder when Mr. Ban

Ki-moon and the international community are going to surprise us with a UN plan of action to immediately, with no further ado, put an end to this illegal occupation which is, as they put it, "contrary to international law."

However, we were pleasantly surprised by the report of the UN Human Rights Council, released at the end of January 2013, which for the first time urged governments and private corporations across the world to consider economic and political sanctions against Israel over its construction of settlements. But this does not mean anything to Israel, who refused to attend the meetings of the Council. In fact, not only does Israel show no respect for any U.N. resolutions or reports, it reacts viciously to them, expanding settlements and demolishing yet more homes. It was heart-wrenching to watch two homes being demolished on February 5, 2013 in the Jerusalem suburbs of Beit Hanina and Anata, as residents and their possessions were thrown out into the cold weather. In an interview on Palestinian TV the next day, Adnan Husseini, the Palestinian minister for Jerusalem, sounded completely frustrated at the scene of those demolished homes with more than 37 persons, mostly children, in the apartment building in Beit Hanina losing their homes. He described Israel as a moving bulldozer trying to bulldoze all the Palestinians out of Jerusalem. The children had all gone to school, and the men were at work when the women of those apartments were faced with the bulldozers that pulled down doors and windows without giving the people a chance to gather their belongings. The children returned from school to find a devastating site: a pile of rubble replacing their homes.

State violence under various pretexts, mostly in the name of "security," continues ceaselessly. So long as the occupation prevails it is not surprising that violence will continue to erupt. And if Israel continues to assert Jerusalem as the united capital of Israel, I think we are living in false hope. We need a just peace, and Jerusalem will be at the center of this peace. But the situation on the ground has become almost irreversible. All efforts on behalf of the PNA to salvage the situation will be "mission impossible" unless the international community intervenes. The renowned Israeli peace activist, Uri Avnery, in his article about Romney and Netanyahu on September 21, 2012, says that nothing is irreversible except death. I hope he is right.

On Yom Kippur, September 18, 2010, when Jews read the words of Prophet Isaiah, "This is the fast that God desires: to unlock the fetters of wickedness, to share your bread with the hungry, to take the wretched poor into your home," I kept wondering what Mr. Netanyahu would be reflecting on that Yom Kippur? Would he make a commitment to justice and peace? Would peace be a priority in his prayers? Or would he give in to the settlers and evict the "wretched Palestinians" from their land and homes, in accordance with the wish of his Foreign Minister, Avigdor Lieberman, and of Chief Rabbi Ovadia Yosef? This Rabbi prayed to God on the Jewish New Year, asking for the Palestinians to be hit by the plague and perish. This is a dream Mr. Netanyahu might also share, but not able to utter, as he is a politician. In fact, the Gush Shalom (Peace Bloc) ad for that week specifically challenged Mr. Netanyahu to choose between the settlements and peace. Gush Shalom used the settlement of Ariel in the heart of the West Bank as an example: "Peace Without Ariel Or Ariel Without Peace. What Do You Choose?" Raiding Jenin and Tulkarm during that period certainly did not bode well for peace; or maybe the incursion was planned in order to give Mr. Netanyahu time to repent before the day was over, and thus start the new year with a clean slate. Israel would certainly need years, not days, of fasting and prayers to atone for all the injustice and suffering of the ongoing *Nakba* of the Palestinians.

It did not take long to know what Mr. Netanyahu chose. It was a few days after Yom Kippur when settlers in Silwan, protected by Israeli police, started another wave of provocation, and clashes erupted between them and the Palestinian youth. During these clashes a private security guard from the settlement shot dead a Palestinian youth, Samer Sarhan. Silwan is not the only site of such incidents; Al-Essawieyeh, al-Tour, Ras el Amoud, Anata, all suburbs around Jerusalem, have been subjected to similar Israeli harassment, clashes, and home demolition. And in response to the UN vote on November 29, 2012 for the status of Palestine as non-member state, a new wave of settlements in area E1, the corridor between the settlement of Maale Adumim and Jerusalem, was announced. Al-Karameh also was not left in peace, and the Bedouins living in that area have been evicted as well. In response, Palestinians erected an innovative village, Bab El-Shams, on the area so brutally attacked by the Israeli army, asserting their right to return to and claim sovereignty over the land.

Residency and Family Reunification

Another form of the onslaught on Jerusalem is the deprivation of family reunification. The process of acquiring permits, or renewing permits for couples seeking family reunification, is subject to endless delay without any explanation. When one of the spouses in a marriage is from outside the Jerusalem area, a permit is required to allow the couple to live together. And when a new baby is born in Jerusalem, parents need to prove that they are actually living in Jerusalem by presenting a whole set of documents, including municipal taxes, electricity, telephone, and sewage bills, etc., in order to be able to register the child. An identity card is not considered enough proof.

I remember when Omar, my first grandson, was born during the early days of the first *Intifada*. The army came knocking at our door and I was so scared, fearing that Israeli soldiers were again coming for my son Suhail, who had been recently released from prison. It turned out they were accompanying the staff of the National Insurance on their visit to my daughter's house on the lower floor of our house to ensure that she was actually living there with the baby. With Omar's clothes hung on the laundry rack inside the house, there was no mistaking the fact that a baby was living in that house. When we asked the staff of the National Insurance about the need to have the army accompany them on their visit, they justified it by saying that they were in "*Intifada* Land."

Very often the staff of the National Insurance would raid homes in the middle of the night to be sure that the people were actually living in the Jerusalem home where they claimed to live. They would open closets and the fridge to check that the place was actually lived in, and would check the bed covers to be sure that the beds were being used. Every family has a story of its own about thwarted family reunification; we too have not been spared. Both spouses of my children are from outside Jerusalem, and the request for their family reunification is an ongoing process that seems as endless as the peace process itself. I continue to hope that this nightmare will soon be over and that my children will be able to live a normal family life. But under a military occupation, it is difficult to hope for a normal life. Fortunately, my daughter-in-law, at least, has a long-term permit that allows her to live with her husband in Jerusalem. However, the situation is different for my daughter and her family. When my husband built a house for them in Birzeit, before the Oslo Accords, the Palestinian territories were all one area. After Oslo, when Jerusalem was closed to people from the West Bank, my daughter and her three children had to stay in Jerusalem for fear of losing their right of residency. My son-in-law, who lives in Birzeit, is hardly ever granted a permit to stay in Jerusalem, and when he is, it is usually for a limited period of time. As a result, my daughter, like so many others, is what we call a weekend wife.

Challenges

Jerusalem schools as well as organizations have not been spared either. The various pressures imposed on them are intended to make their presence in Jerusalem irrelevant, or to force them out of the city. Even cultural activities and festivals have become a great challenge for organizations and their sponsors, who continue to face obstacles imposed by military orders. When Israel, which claims to be a leading country in the world of arts, deprives a small community from the pleasure of enjoying music or a literature festival, then there is something very wrong in the psyche of those occupying forces. Perhaps Israel would rather see us blowing up buses, so that it would have a good reason to lock us up or expel us from the country. But by our summud (steadfastness) we shall defend our freedom and rights, using music, art, drama, literature, and any other non-violent and creative means of resistance. In fact, the summer issues of This Week in Palestine magazine, with its listing of various activities, is proof enough that Palestinian society is still a vibrant society, enjoying activities, art exhibits, and festivals not only in Jerusalem, but also in Ramallah, Birzeit, Nablus, Jenin and other parts of the country. Even in Gaza, which is under siege, the Edward Said National Conservatory was able to start running the music school there in the fall of 2012; the children enjoy the school tremendously.

While we continue to be creative in cultural activities, to practice summud as a way to overcome the pressures of occupation, Israel, with its diabolical penchant for oppression, never fails to conjure up the most innovative measures to subdue the Jerusalemites. It is making life extremely difficult for Palestinians in order to encourage their emigration, or at least to limit their presence to a minimum percentage of its population. Meanwhile, the Israeli population has increased, due to the annexation of the Israeli settlements built on Palestinian land never before included in the city of Jerusalem.

The "Wall" has already excluded a large percentage of Jerusalem's Palestinian residents, and so has the Israeli withdrawal of the right of residency of students who studied abroad and did not return home in time to renew their permits, or those who married spouses from outside the city. There are thousands of children who are now deprived of living with both parents because of this phenomenon. Now the Jerusalem municipality is considering relinquishing its responsibility over the Jerusalem neighborhoods that fall outside the separation wall to the "civil" administration of the military occupation. Taking into consideration that the Palestinian National Authority (PNA) is not allowed into these neighborhoods, this means that the residents of those neighborhoods will live in the bizarre situation created by Israel, "neither here nor there."

Even the Arabic names of the city and its streets have not been spared this ongoing onslaught. Israel is renaming historic streets, buildings, and sites with Hebrew names, so as to obliterate not only our existence but our history and heritage, Ironically, however, in Arab neighborhoods such as Beit Hanina and Shufaat the Israeli municipality has been giving Arabic names to side streets and small alleys that never had names before. As a result, now we have minor streets named after Arab luminaries such as the famous writer Mai Ziadeh and the well-known singer Um Kulthum. Meanwhile, however, our request to name the street that leads to our house after the name of my late husband Yousef has been ignored ever since we requested this after his death. Yousef not only opened that street in the early sixties but also developed and planted trees in all the projects that he built in that area, such as the Helen Keller School and the Rosary Sisters convent. As chairman of the Arab Housing Society he was also the driving force behind the building of two housing projects for the Palestinian families of Jerusalem very close to that area. Yet despite all his contributions to the area we have been unable to get permission to give the street his name.

Just as ironic is the VIP service that is granted to the residents of Jerusalem for a high fee. This service, despite its cost, makes the crossing to Amman and back much easier than the nightmare it used to be. I was there towards the end of January 2013, and I could not believe the difference, not only with regard to the procedure that I wrote about in an earlier chapter, but also with regard to the people working there. At the Israeli crossing point I was asked by one of the attendants if I would like to drink something. As I sat there, stunned, she further asked, "coffee, tea?" I have problems in hearing, so I wondered: was I hearing correctly? Is she really offering me something to drink? "No thank you," I responded politely. While she took my fees to get me the permit I could not help but wonder. Could these be the same people who used to practically "bark" at us giving us orders to sit and move and strip, put our shoes on top of the pile, etc.? If that attendant had been at the Qalandia checkpoint, would she be as gracious? How can human beings switch personalities from one situation to another and maintain their sanity? It reminded me of Stevensons's strange story of Dr. Jeckyll and Mr. Hyde.

But I cannot deny that I was pleasantly surprised that my encounter was with the good Dr. Jeckyll. I got my permit, and my bag was carried by a porter who escorted me to a private shuttle that drove me to the Jordanian point. At the Jordanian point, my bag was not checked for "Israeli products or publications." In no time I was out and on my way to Amman. From my house in Beit Hanina to my cousin's house in the Abdoun area in Amman it took only two hours. I was still in a daze, remembering those 7-10 hours of crossing. On the way back the journey was just as easy. There was no searching, stripping or having to take off our shoes; and despite the long lines of buses coming back from the "Omrah" (the small pilgrimage to Mecca), I was on the platform to pick up a taxi home in no time.

Was this part of the Oslo Accords? Or was this part of an economic agreement whereby the VIP service has become a business concern? Will the comfort of business agreements make us forget the ugly face of the occupation? But the brutal measures of the Occupying forces do not give anybody a chance to forget. I remember how during the early years of the occupation, the business people were the last to cooperate with the civil society when we needed them to rally for action in resisting the occupation. Their vested interests were always a priority. That is why it is very painful, and indeed, unacceptable, to see some Jerusalemites, especially our religious leaders, enjoying refreshments at receptions hosted by the president of Israel or by the mayor of Jerusalem as if life was normal in the city, while our homes are being demolished and our prisoners are on hunger strike. The occupation has not come to an end yet, and the issue of Jerusalem has not yet been solved.

There was a time when Israel offered the Arab residents of Jerusalem Israeli passports, but Faisal Husseini advised against it. Every option or offer we ever had under this occupation was a two-edged sword. Perhaps Israel at the time wanted to prove to the world that there are no Palestinians in Jerusalem by turning them into Israeli citizens. Of course some people made use of this offer, especially merchants and people who were working inside Israel. Yet most Palestinians categorically refused the offer. Now, in retrospect, I keep wondering whether that was the correct choice. Since we could not beat them, maybe we could have outnumbered them. Israel is haunted by the Palestinian demographic threat, and it continues to create laws to limit the number of Palestinians in Jerusalem. It hopes in this way to maintain the Jewish identity of the city. However, if peace is to prevail in the region, Jerusalem, the cradle of all three faiths, Judaism, Christianity and Islam, can never be an exclusive city.

Maybe it was divine intervention that Faisal was spared this onslaught on Jerusalem. It would have grieved him deeply. His loss is the loss of a guiding beacon. Yet his spirit continues to be present through the Faisal Husseini Foundation, which supports schools as well as health and cultural institutions in Jerusalem. His children, Abed El-Qader and Fadwa, are heavily involved in the work of the Foundation.

While The Orient House in Jerusalem was a point of reference for Palestinian resistance during those long years of the occupation, my generation also remembers it as a hotel with an open air-dancing floor. When Yousef and I were courting in the late fifties we enjoyed many summer evenings there, as well as at the Grand Hotel in Ramallah, dancing freely to the beautiful melodies of Italian or Spanish bands, tangos, waltzes, passé-doubles, and even rock n roll, the popular dance music for the youth at the time. I dream of past joys, and continue to hope that the generation of my grandchildren, at least, will be able to have lovely memories of this city, when someday it truly becomes the city of peace.

Futile Negotiations

One of the basic flaws of the Oslo accords, among many, was deferring the issue of Jerusalem, along with the other major issues of the right of return of the refugees, borders, and the future of the settlements, to the final stage of negotiations at the end of a five year period.

Now that the five year period has been four times over, I cannot help but draw an analogy with a conversation I had with my mother in 1980, after we had received a letter from my daughter Dina, who was studying nursing in London. The first ward she was allocated to for her training was the geriatrics ward. In her letter she was describing how tough it was to deal with the elderly people. My mother commented that it must be very wise of the hospital administration to let the nursing students go through this in their early training. She was sure that if they could survive geriatrics, they would be able to make it into the profession and be able to cope with the rest of the training in the various hospital wards.

Yes indeed, had those tough core issues been tackled right at the beginning, it would have been a sure test as to whether the negotiations were viable and could lead to the Peace that we all yearned for. Instead, while the first five years were supposed to be devoted to building trust, Israel spent those years building settlements.

Dina training at St. Thomas' in London

By 2011 the landscape of the occupied territories was completely changed. After eighteen years of futile negotiations—direct, indirect, or in proximity—there was a new reality on the ground. The PNA, which had stopped peace negotiations with Israel after the brutal Operation Cast Lead attack on the Gaza Strip at the end of 2008, was adamant that it would not return to the negotiating table before Israel stopped the building of settlements, especially in Jerusalem. Yet again and again the PNA was coerced into returning to negotiations.

When Israel announced in November 2009 that it was going to build 900 housing units in Gilo settlement, it was very encouraging to read the many comments in the papers and on the Internet deploring that move. Gilo was established on land belonging to the town of Beit Jala (in the Bethlehem area) that was illegally confiscated and annexed to Jerusalem. But deploring, regretting, reprimanding and being dismayed do not make any difference if no serious action or sanctions are imposed.

Even President Obama got a slap in the face when he attempted to order Israel to stop building settlements in September 2010. Not only did Israel defy his order, but by doing so, Israel also sent a message to the world community that nobody can order it around, not even the US administration. What audacity, when Israel would not have been created or survived without the support of the US administration, nor would it have been able to maintain its military occupation of the Palestinian, Lebanese and Syrian territories since 1967. But when a spoilt child is allowed to get away with anything for decades, such impudence should not come as a surprise.

Eventually the PNA caved in. However, to save face, it only accepted to resume proximity talks. These started in May 2010. Mr. Mitchell once again started flying to the region, shuttling between West Jerusalem and Ramallah. For three months nothing came of those talks. Our long experience with negotiations since the Oslo Accords did not give us reason to expect anything new. This is why we were quite cynical and angry when it was announced on August

21, 2010 that direct talks would resume on September 2, and why we tried to protest. We could not accept the justification given for resuming those talks when the reason for halting the negotiations in the first place remained firmly in place, and when the reality on the ground was deteriorating faster than ever.

However, the choice was between refusing to engage in negotiations, or losing the aid money that kept the PNA and the whole system including its thousands of employees surviving. The irony is that the oppressed are being black mailed by the threat of having aid stopped, while the oppressors and perpetrators of international law—the Israelis—are being rewarded with further aid. Palestinian President Abbas announced that he would withdraw from the talks should the freeze on settlement expansion be lifted on the 26th of September, 2010, though he knew very well that he was in no position to set ultimatums. Ironically, there was never a real freeze on settlement building. One such example, out of hundreds that took place during the talks, was the Israeli confiscation and development of large areas of Al-Walaja land near Beit Jala.

Eventually Mr. Abbas, the architect of Oslo, and the chief negotiator, Saeb Uraiqat, realized the futility of those negotiations. We keep wondering what took them so long, when the Palestinian people realized this much sooner. In fact I keep wondering whether the PNA will ever have the courage to take the risk of refusing to engage in those negotiations, despite the consequences. At least to maintain its dignity and the respect and confidence of its people, which have been completely eroded. It would certainly be a real test for the Arab world as well. The Arab countries have enough resources to foot the bill of the PNA if they are genuinely concerned about the plight of the Palestinians and especially about Jerusalem. We have heard plenty of rhetoric and slogans about Jerusalem being in their hearts, but we have not seen anything to prove that "their money is where their heart is" (Mathew 6:21).

My personal reaction to the talks was inspired by the Arabic saying "We tell you it's a bull, and you insist that we milk it." How can a bull be milked? And how can we get anything out of negotiations when Israel is willing to offer nothing in the first place? In fact, while Mr. Abbas was consulting with the PLO Executive Committee and the Fateh Central Committee, as well as with the Follow Up Arab Committee (which was to meet in Cairo on October 4, 2010), to look into the possibility of resuming the negotiations, the Israeli supreme court issued an order on September 28 approving the eviction of tens of families from their homes in the Sheikh Jarrah quarter of East Jerusalem. In the meantime, Mr. Mitchel came to Jerusalem in an effort to salvage the peace negotiations.

Once again, Mr. Obama asked Israel to freeze the settlements. At the same time he urged the Arabs, just as Mrs. Clinton had done a few years ago, to take courageous steps to normalize relations with Israel. If Israel is really keen on peace, however, it does not need further talks; it would simply withdraw from the occupied territories. The Arab Peace Initiative offered to Israel at the Arab Summit meeting in Lebanon in 2002 was very clear in stipulating that all Arab and Muslim Countries would be willing to normalize their relations with Israel if it were to withdraw from the occupied territories. If it were possible to change the reality of Palestine overnight in 1948, it certainly should be possible to get the Israeli forces and their settlers out of the occupied territories.

The Arabs have already taken that courageous step that Mrs. Clinton has been urging them to take. But the problem is that Israel turned a cold shoulder to the Arab Peace Initiative; and unfortunately the Palestinian leadership has not continued to remind the world community about that initiative. Even if this initiative is not ideal, it seems the only possible solution, should there still be resolve for the realization of two states. Israel could not have had a better offer to guarantee its security as part of the Middle East region.

At the opening in Washington of the talks for resuming negotiations, both Mr. Obama and Mrs. Clinton commended the parties for getting together, and emphasized the parties' responsibility to solve matters. If the US had no intention to pressure Israel, however, then why did they drag the whole fanfare to Washington? The Palestinians were pressured, or rather blackmailed, by the threat that funding would be cut off should President Abbas refuse to engage in direct talks. But there was no threat made to Israel that American aid to Israel would be cut should Israel refuse the request of the US to stop building settlements.

Diana Buttu, a Palestinian Canadian lawyer and former spokesperson for the PLO, emphasizes the hypocrisy of this US double standard: "While the U.S. advocates (and even fights for) the return of Bosnian and East Timorese refugees, Palestinian rights are extinguished by the U.S.; while the U.S. claims that it supports civil rights, the U.S. also supports a state that advocates superior rights for a certain class of people; while the U.S. is opposed to the taking of property without compensation, it supports regime after regime in Israel who make no secret of the fact that they have stolen property in the past and will continue to do so in the future." [17]

This double standard is also evident in the race for nuclear armament. While the US special envoy to North Korea commented that Pyongyang's claim of a new uranium enrichment facility is provocative and disappointing, we have never heard a single comment from the US declaring its disappointment in Israel's nuclear facilities. In fact, Israel is threatening to wage a war on Iran under the pretext that it is a threat to Israeli security. Ironically, the uranium enrichment of Iran has been subject to inspection, while Israel, the only country in the Middle East that actually has nuclear facilities, does not allow inspectors into its facilities. Should Israel drag the US into a war against Iran, the US cannot but blame itself for reaping what it has been sowing for years.

A friend of mine returned from a trip to the post office in October 2012 to report that Israel was distributing gas masks, presumably in preparation for a war with Iran. I still remember how in 1991, during the Gulf War, gas masks were available only to Israelis and

---

17 See The Institute for Middle East Understanding, "*The Nakba: Then and Now,*" May 15, 2006. http://imeu.net/news/article001375.shtml

to residents of East Jerusalem, not to West Bank Palestinians. We hesitated greatly before collecting masks for ourselves, realizing that my sister and my brother and so many others could not access them. However, for the sake of the grandchildren we finally got the masks and prepared a sealed room. After we were all inside and had settled down, I remembered the birdcage, which we had to go and fetch. Then as soon as we were settled again, I remembered the seeds for the bird. "Now what?" yelled Yousef, when he realized what I was going out for. "Did you think we were staying here for a month?" The children still make fun of me for this. But after all that hassle, we hardly stayed in the room at all; eventually we watched the Scud missiles from the roof of our house.

Looking back at the negotiations, it is clear that not only did Mr. Netanyahu refuse to extend the freeze on the Israeli settlements after direct negotiations had restarted in Washington, he literally challenged the US president by announcing the building of 1,300 settler units while on his way to Washington to meet Vice President Biden and Secretary of State Clinton.

In the meantime, while we were commemorating forty-four years of Israeli occupation (as of June 5, 2011) and sixty-three years of dispossession, France came up with a new/old initiative: an international conference to be followed by negotiations. If this was going to be another Madrid, our feeling was, "Thank you France, but no thank you. We had not forgotten all that happened after the Madrid Conference, and the negotiations that ensued; we had a feeling that this was but another initiative to preempt the Palestinian plan to seek recognition at the United Nations in September 2011. It was clear that the only thing that would come out of that conference initiative would be further stalling, further realities on the ground, a further onslaught on Jerusalem and further intransigence on the Israeli side. Mr. Netanyahu, who insisted on resuming negotiations without pre-conditions, himself set seven conditions: no to the 1967 borders, no negotiations on Jerusalem, no return of refugees, no dismantling of settlements, no withdrawal from the Jordan Valley;

no peace without recognition of the Jewishness of the State, and no arms for the Palestinian State. We heard them all as he addressed the American Congress with 29 standing ovations, something he doesn't get even at home, in his own Knesset.

Every time negotiations have reached the stage of dealing with any of the core issues that have been deferred, Israel has balked. So are the Palestinians expected to get on the merry-go-round again? We have already been there, and as the Arabic saying goes, "A person cannot be bitten twice from the serpent's pit." Unfortunately, however, the PNA continued to reach into the serpent's pit until eventually it decided, out of desperation and frustration, to take its case to the UN.

It was only a few years ago, in 2007, that UNRWA (the United Nations Relief and Works Agency) met at the Dead Sea to discuss its financial crisis and the deficit in its budget for providing services to Palestinian refugees. UNRWA was established as a temporary agency for the relief of 750,000 Palestinian refugees after 1948. After fifty-nine years it certainly is not temporary any more. Its mission would have been much more fruitful, both financially and morally, had the United Nations enforced its resolutions regarding the right of return of those refugees, rather than create a humanitarian issue out of it. Under the circumstances, we continue to be thankful for the UN and its commitment to humanitarian aid, as expressed by Mr. Kevin Kennedy, the UN Humanitarian Coordinator for the Occupied Palestinian Territories. However, the Palestinian issue has been dealt with as a humanitarian and refugee issue for too long. Yes, we need assistance to survive; but we also need our political rights and a state of our own, so that we can maintain our dignity and identity without having to plead for handouts forever. Continuing to provide humanitarian aid is one way of acquiescing to the ongoing reality of Palestinian refugee camps and of relieving Israel from its responsibility as an occupying force.

The UN bid for recognition brought about a great deal of discussion, statements, articles and political analysis from all aspects: legal, moral and otherwise. The discussion covered the pros and cons, the dilemmas and opportunities, the hope and despair, the disappointment and futility that have long plagued the Palestinian issue. It was clear that there was no consensus even amongst Palestinians regarding that initiative. How could the body that created the problem by unfairly partitioning Palestine in 1948, and which has failed ever since to force Israel to implement a single UN resolution pertaining to Palestinian rights, be entrusted with the realization of the Palestinian dream of liberation and independence? How could it be viewed as credible? It is understandable that many Palestinians, especially those in the *shatat* (diaspora) and in internal refugee camps, would be worried that the inalienable rights of Palestinians, especially their right of return, would not be realized, or that the Palestinian state, if and when recognized, would be far removed from the Palestinian dream of justice. Amidst all this controversy, I found myself inspired by Shakespeare's Hamlet and his famous question, "To be or not to be, that is the question." I conjured alternative lines to this famous speech, lines that reflected the realities at stake in the UN Bid:

To go or not to go, that is the question
Whether to suffer the measures of occupation
The outrageous checkpoints and wall of separation
Whether to indulge in futile negotiations
Or take our case to the United Nations
To go or not to go is no more the question

Once Mr. Abbas and his entourage were already at the UN, to go or not to go to the United Nations was no more the question. Mr. Abbas submitted his bid to the Secretary General on Friday the 23rd of September 2011. He then delivered his address, a comprehensive address that hardly left any issue untouched. For the first time since the negotiations started he said everything that should have been said many years ago. Of course, his speech did not obliterate the controversy amongst Palestinians about this initiative, and many still had reason to worry about the inalienable rights of the Palestinians, and the futility of submitting the bid to the Security Council instead of the General Assembly. With the long history of American veto, the UN bid seemed like a lost effort from the start; and indeed, the effort stalled. However, there was so much applause during Mr. Abbas' address that it seemed that there might have been a chance for passing a vote at the General Assembly to change the status of Palestine from an observer entity to an observer state. Other than the moral support, however, such a change would not change our reality. This reality was clearly expressed in the arrogance with which Mr. Netanyahu responded to the speech of Mr. Abbas: the contempt he displayed was shameful, although not surprising.

A year later the Palestinians announced again that they were going to seek recognition at the United Nations as an observer state. It was simply a matter of timing, because of the American elections. However, the US Ambassador to the UN, Ms. Susan Rice, announced that such a move would jeopardize the peace process, and that "any efforts to use international fora to prejudge final status issues that can only be resolved directly by the parties will neither improve the daily lives of Palestinians nor foster the trust essential to make progress towards a two state solution." How can a bid at the UN jeopardize the peace process which has been stalling for 19 years, and which, according to some Israeli as well as Palestinian and international writers and analysts, is already "DEAD"? I hope Ms. Rice can see that what has jeopardized the peace process, and continues to do so, is the intransigence of Israel and the new reality it has created in the occupied territories, especially the separation Wall, the confiscation of land, the building of settlements, and the demolition of homes. Those realities have already prejudged the final status issues.

The situation has deteriorated to such an extent that it has become clear that oppressed people should never negotiate with their oppressors, unless they are strong enough to do so. Through its power and money Israel has been calling all the shots.

To understand why Israel has so strongly opposed any UN initiative, we need to remember that Israel has never acknowledged the West Bank, East Jerusalem and the Gaza Strip as occupied territories. The International Court of Justice, the highest interpreter of International Law, ruled unequivocally in 2004 that the West Bank is indeed an Occupied Territory, actually "occupied" by Israel. Israel first considered these territories "liberated," and later, when negotiations started after the 1993 Oslo Accords, referred to them as "disputed territories." Meanwhile, the borders of East Jerusalem were extended and unilaterally annexed, and were thereby placed outside the discussion altogether. The scenario that Israel projected allowed it to claim that it had acquired the territory fair and square in a war that the Arab countries waged against Israel in 1967, despite the fact that Israeli sources clearly demonstrate Israeli responsibility for the war through its preemptive strike on Egypt. For instance, according to Miko Peled, the son of Matti Peled, an Israeli general during the war of 1967, his father "clearly stated that contrary to claims made later, the 1967 war was one of choice."[18] However, that is neither the first or last myth that Israel has propagated in its narrative justifying the grabbing of Palestinian land. The main reason given, over and above all, is that of the divine right that Israel claims over the whole land of Palestine. Based on this belief, Israel considers that it is the one making very hard concessions by giving the Palestinians a part of its land, "Eretz Yisrael." The latest report, released in July 2012 by a committee formed by Prime Minister Netanyahu and headed by former Supreme Court Justice Edmond Levy to examine the legal status of West Bank land ownership, rejects the claim that Israel's presence in the territory is that of an occupying force, and instead asserts that its settlements and settlement outposts there are legal according to international law.

18   Iris Keltz, on http://mikopeled.com/. Miko Peled, in his book *The General's Son*, quotes General Peled regarding the truth about Israel's preemptive strike against Egypt that started the June 6, 1967 war. See pp. 43-44.

It is worth noting that the British Mandate in Palestine (1917-1948) used the Hebrew initials "Eretz Yisrael" on Palestinian passports as well as on the Palestinian currency. The word Palestine appeared in the three languages, English, Arabic, and Hebrew; however, next to Palestine in the Hebrew translation was the addition of the initials "EY." In a devious way, that confirmed the plan of the British Mandate for the implementation of the Balfour Declaration on all the Palestinian Land. The Balfour Declaration of November 2, 1917, a letter from the British Foreign Secretary Arthur James Balfour to Baron Rothschild, a leader of the British Jewish community, for transmission to the Zionist Federation of Great Britain and Ireland. It stated:

His Majesty's government views with favour the establishment in Palestine of a national home for the Jewish people, and will use their best endeavours to facilitate the achievement of this object, it being clearly understood that nothing shall be done which may prejudice the civil and religious rights of existing non-Jewish communities in Palestine, or the rights and political status enjoyed by Jews in any other country.

Given all the new realities that Israel has created on the ground through the government and army-supported settlements, it is clear that in fact everything, rather than nothing, was done "*to prejudice and violate the civil and religious rights of the Palestinians.*" And it has become obvious beyond any doubt that Israel is not interested in peace. Instead, it is taking all the necessary measures to make it impossible for the creation of a Palestinian state along side the state of Israel.

It seems clear that if Israel continues to stall, a new, irreversible reality of one state between the Jordan River and the Mediterranean will prevail. This has always been the dream of the Palestinians, as well as the ideal solution. But Israel will then have to face the dilemma of choosing between being a democracy for all its citizens or an apartheid state. In the meantime, it will make life very difficult, indeed almost unbearable, for the Palestinians, so as to encourage the largest number possible to leave the country. However, if Israel is hoping to deal with the Palestinians simply as a demography problem, it is in for a surprise. Despite the emigration that has been taking place, the general sentiment among Palestinians is a determination to stay put, despite the difficulty of doing so, and to face challenges with dignity.

What was really puzzling and disappointing was the reaction of the US administration to the UN bid. If the US were genuinely interested in peace and stability in the region as well as in the security of Israel—which President Obama, like previous presidents, continues to emphasize as a priority for US policy—the US administration should be the first to approve the principle of a Palestinian state. Actually, it is worth reminding Mr. Obama that in his speech at the United Nations in September 2010 he said, *"The world can have an agreement that will lead to the creation of a new Palestinian state next year."* He must have forgotten his words, because without even seeing the details of the Palestinian bid, or trying to forge that agreement that he spoke of, Mr. Obama sent two of his envoys, Mr. Dennis Ross and Mr. David Hale, to convince Mr. Abbas to change his mind about the UN bid. Why? Mr. Abbas was humiliated enough in the negotiations. Every time he threatened, and rightly so, not to return to the negotiating table, the US administration intervened. For the sake of peace, the Palestinians have been humiliated and forced to make many concessions at the expense of their rights. According to the New York Times, "Matti Steinberg, a former senior adviser to Israeli security chiefs, described Mr. Abbas as the most obliging, nonviolent Palestinian leader Israel has encountered, and warned of taking him for granted. 'The Israeli center is caught in a vicious cycle,' he said. 'It argues that it cannot make peace while there is violence, and when there is no violence it sees little reason to make peace.'" [19]

---

19 *New York Times*, Sunday Review, June 22, 2012.

However, Mr. Obama lost more credibility as a potential peace broker, when he rushed into signing the United States-Israel Enhanced Security Cooperation Act on the eve of Romney's visit to Israel at the end of July 2012, with further aid of $70 million to develop its Iron Dome missile defense system. What a difference from Mr. Obama's inaugural address in 2009, which radiated hope and resolve for change[20]. When Mr. Obama was awarded the Nobel Peace Prize, it was probably the first time anyone had been awarded a peace prize a priori for his rhetoric instead of for his achievements.

Unfortunately, the European Union seemed to be rewarding Israel as well when it announced, on 27 July 2012, that it would strengthen its bilateral relations with Israel by endorsing a package of 60 new areas of cooperation. Amnesty International, however, added its voice to that of Palestinians, who expressed their disappointment. According to AI, the EU decision was taken without giving due consideration to ongoing violations of international human rights and humanitarian law in Israel and the occupied Palestinian territories. Nicolas Beger, Director of Amnesty International's European Institutions Office, stated that "International human rights and humanitarian obligations should be at the centre of EU relations with all countries, including Israel," and that "Enhancing relations whilst the EU's own demands and benchmarks are not being met is a clear case of double standards and sends the wrong message."

Needless to say, this UN bid was stalemated, like so many efforts Palestine has made in seeking legitimacy and recognition. However, shortly after that great disappointment, Palestine was admitted with flying flags on October 31, 2011 to UNESCO, the United Nations Educational, Scientific and Cultural Organization. Even France voted yes, perhaps to make up for not taking a positive stand regarding the UN Bid. And in July 2012 the Church of the Nativity and the pilgrimage route in Bethlehem, Palestine were inscribed on the UNESCO World Heritage list. Although these seemed symbolic

---

20 My letter to Mr. Obama after his inaugural speech appears in Appendix VIII.

gestures, for Palestinians who have been deprived of recognition as a people and as a country, these achievements boosted our morale. We were especially encouraged since the reconciliation between Fateh and Hamas was making progress, and everybody hoped that elections would take place soon. Unfortunately, just as the Central Elections Committee had begun its work in Gaza, and despite the fact that things were going smoothly, the CEC was ordered by the leadership in Gaza to stop further work. Not only was the committee itself disappointed; so too was the whole population, because this reflected negatively on the reconciliation initiative. Municipality elections on the West Bank alone did eventually take place on October 20, 2012. In February 2013 the CEC was permitted to resume its work in Gaza, at the same time as reconciliation talks between Fateh and Hamas and the various Palestinians factions regarding the restructuring of the PLO were taking place in Cairo.

In January 2012, about the time that the futile negotiations—direct talks, indirect talks, proximity talks—ran out of terminology to portray them, Jordan, to everybody's great surprise, and with no justification, hosted a new round of talks between the Israelis and the Palestinians. These were called exploratory talks, as if to pull the wool over our eyes; after all, the PNA had already announced more than once that no negotiations would resume as long as the building of settlements continued.

This time the talks took place in the presence of the Quartet (the United Nations, the United States, the European Union, and Russia), the chief Palestinian negotiator, and the Israeli negotiator, in order to explore the question of how the negotiations could start again. "How" was never the issue, however; the real issue was "when" and "if" the building of settlements would come to a halt. Once again the Palestinian people were being taken for a ride while something serious was being cooked up behind their backs. On January 14, 2012, people demonstrated in front of the headquarters of the Palestinian National Authority in Ramallah, protesting the endless and futile negotiations that had brought nothing but more disastrous realities on the ground. It was unacceptable, and very sad, when Palestinian police brutally attacked Palestinians protesting the visit of Shaul Mofaz, vice prime minister and chairman of Kadima, to Ramallah in June 2012. Mofaz had been the Israeli Chief of Staff during the eruption of the second *Intifada* and during the brutal and bloody raid on the Jenin camp in 2002.

On November 29, 2012, the PNA again sought recognition at the UN, and this time the General Assembly voted overwhelmingly to recognize Palestine as a non-member state. The 193-member assembly voted 138 in favor of the recognition, with only nine against and 41 abstentions. It was not surprising to watch the US and Israel vote against the resolution, but their vote left them in the minority block.

As critical as many of us have been of how the negotiations were carried out, we all rejoiced at the vote, just as much as we rejoiced at the belated release of the pre-Oslo prisoners by installments, irrespective of the circumstances.

As I write this, I have hopes that the meetings of the various Palestinian factions for restructuring the PLO and the reconciliation begun in Cairo on February 9, 2013 will materialize, and that elections will take place. However, we have to remember that Palestinians in the occupied territories do not represent all the Palestinians around the world. In order for there to be any hope for determining the future of a Palestinian State with Al-Quds as its capital there must be elections for the Palestinian National Council (PNC) as well, and these elections must include all the Palestinians, both inside Palestine and in the *Shatat* (diaspora).

In Solidarity

Although the Oslo Accords provided for release of prisoners, many of the prisoners who were supposed to be released are still languishing in Israeli jails, with new arrests made every day. Some prisoners were released through prisoner exchange deals, including one on October 18, 2011 in which Palestinian prisoners were exchanged for Gila'd Shalit, the Israeli soldier captured by Hamas in a cross-border raid near Gaza on June 25, 2006. Yet a number of the released Palestinians are now back in jail under different pretexts. The Jerusalem parliamentarians who won in the 2006 elections on the Hamas ballot have been continuously threatened with deportation orders. For almost two years they held a sit-in at the Red Cross in Jerusalem to avoid deportation; the community showed solidarity with their protest by joining in the sit-in. On January 23, 2012, the Israeli police in Jerusalem abducted two of these parliamentarians, Khaled Abu Arafeh, who was also the former Minister of Jerusalem affairs, and Mohammad Taha. (Israel claims that they were not on the Red Cross premises when they were arrested. Perhaps they were simply taking a stroll in the narrow alley in front of the Red Cross.) A week earlier, Israeli police had arrested the speaker of the Palestinian Parliament, Aziz Duweik, who has been in and out of jail ever since he was elected. Hopefully his release on July 20, 2012 signals his last detention.

In the early months of 2012, the prisoners decided they had had enough, especially those detained without charge or trial. Such detention, which can be indefinitely renewed without any reason provided, is known as "administrative detention." Around 300 Palestinian prisoners are presently held on such basis in Israeli jails, although no charge has been made against them and they have been given no trial. In Feburary 2012 Khadder Adnan, from Arraba in the Jenin area, spearheaded one of the longest hunger strikes, 66 days in length, after he was imprisoned again under administrative detention on January 17. He agreed to put an end to the hunger strike when the Israeli court decided not to renew his detention after his four-month term of imprisonment ended on April 17. Adnan felt it was a "Divine Intervention" that the day of his release coincided with Palestinian Prisoners' Day. But he was not released until very late, after midnight, in the same manner that he had been arrested, also after midnight. Although many of the people who had gathered in the town-square to welcome him back home had given up hope and left, there were still enough people who could by then guess the tactics of the Israeli occupation forces.

Hana' Shalabi from Jenin, who joined the hunger strike and who had already spent two years in administrative detention, was one of those released in the Gila'd Shalit deal. However, that did not give her immunity against another round of administrative detention. After 44 days Israel did not want to be responsible for her demise, so she was released. But instead of sending her back home, she was deported to Gaza in critical condition. Others, including Bilal Diab and Tha'er Halahleh, joined the hunger strike and continued fasting beyond 60 days. It was such a relief for the prisoners' families when it was announced that, due to the deal signed with the prison authority for improved conditions, the prisoners had ended their hunger strike on May 14, 2012. We continue to hope that Israel will actually improve prison conditions. Mahmoud Sarsak, who also joined the hunger strike, got a lot of international publicity and solidarity as his health deteriorated. Sarsak is a football player who was arrested at the Erez crossing as he was travelling from his home in Rafah to join the national team in Balata camp in the Nablus area. He was finally released on July 10, 2012. However, another of the prisoners detained without charge or trial, Samer Issawi, was rushed to the hospital on February 5, 2013 in critical condition after a hunger strike of 197 days. His phenomenal resistance has been widely covered by the media, and on February 4, 2013 a solidarity protest took place in front of the Ramle prison. Parents, grandparents, wives and children gather daily at the Red Cross offices in different parts of the country along with the community, in solidarity with these prisoners. Sadly, however, the world is watching silently while Israel refuses to yield.

Like so many of the absurd laws imposed on Palestinians, the administrative detention law was inherited from the British Emergency Laws during their Mandate over Palestine—as if Israel does not have enough procedures of its own that violate human rights! A concerted effort by prisoners, lawyers and political activists, Palestinian as well as Israeli, is being waged to put an end to this brutal procedure.

The hunger strike of the prisoners evoked the memory of the martyrs of the Nafha prisoners' hunger strike in 1980, Rassem Halaweh from Gaza and Ali Jaafari from Hebron. The women's movement spearheaded ongoing sit-in strikes in solidarity with the families of the prisoners, and my sister Rima wrote a special song at the time in honor of the prisoners of Nafah. In fact, during the years of occupation Rima has been recording the struggle of our people against the occupation, their hopes and aspirations, through her lyrics and music. Several of her songs are recorded on a tape, Ahlamu Shaabi (The dreams of my people) and on a CD, Ila Mata, (Until when), with Soprano Tania Tamari Nasir, our sister-in law. Rima's songs address many instances of Palestinian suffering and

Rima and Tania at the launching of their CD "Ila Mata"

resistance, including the attack on the mayors of Nablus, Ramallah and El-Bireh, when Bassam Shakaa lost his legs and Karim Khalaf was injured in the foot. Rima had a special song for the Hammouri mother who lost two of her children on the same day, and for Hania, her husband's niece who was shot in the leg as she came out of school. Her songs touch upon many other sad stories, including what has happened to Lebanon, and the massacre of Palestinian refugees in the refugee camps of Sabra and Shatilla outside of Beirut. But she has written hopeful songs as well, including a bright one welcoming my son Suhail when he was released from jail. One of the most popular of her songs is the Song of the Bird, dedicated to Palestinian children. It is about a child telling the bird his story of dispossession and pleading with him to teach him how to be free and live in dignity beyond the sound of bullets. (Rima's musical works "Songs of Freedom and Hope" were launched on November 2, 2013)

Despite our disillusion with the negotiations, Palestinians in general have not lost hope that we can and will achieve our rights.

At one of the weekly protests in Bilin against the Wall

We have a just cause that urges us to continue struggling for our rights. Unfortunately, some of the young people, especially those who spent their youth rotting in Israeli jails while deals were being forged at the cost of their rights, have actually lost hope and these days are just minding their own business. Others, however, find it more important than ever to continue the struggle so that their years in jail will not have gone to waste.

With the general consensus for non-violent resistance, more weekly protests are taking place across the country, voicing dissent and taking a stand against the closure of roads, confiscation of land, evictions, and home demolitions. In the face of non-violence, the Israeli army confronts peaceful protesters with tear gas, rubber bullets, and, very often, live ammunition. According to the report from OCHA[21] in August 2012, Israel has allocated 18% of the Palestinian West Bank territory as a closed military area for training purposes.

---

21 UN office for the Coordination of Humanitarian Affairs

However, that has not deterred the Palestinians and the international and Israeli solidarity movements from showing up again and again at weekly protests in towns such as Bilin, Nilin, Walaja, Kufur Eddeek, Kufur Qaddoum, Nabi Saleh, Al-Ma'asarah, Beit Ummar, and many others, as well as at Sheikh Jarrah in East Jerusalem, in the hope that all these efforts will bring about some change.

Actually, the non-violent movement started many years ago with the first *Intifada* in 1988, in Beit Sahour, a small Christian town near Bethlehem. The whole town engaged in civil disobedience. Some residents even burned their Israeli Identity Cards. The harsh measures through which the Israeli forces reacted to this resistance deterred other neighboring towns from following suit. Israeli soldiers attacked homes of activists, toppled food supplies at stores, and mixed oil and soap with flour and rice and other dry ingredients. The course of history might have changed completely had the Beit Sahour model been able to spread to the whole of the West Bank. But it was not humanly possible to stand up to such brutality. However, even this abhorrent treatment did not deter the town from hosting a Palestinian Israeli Rapprochement Centre.

Another form of non-violent resistance has been the BDS (Boycott, Divestment and Sanctions) campaign waged since 2005 by the overwhelming majority of Palestinian civil society, and led since 2008 by the BDS National Committee (BNC), the largest coalition in Palestinian civil society. This campaign calls for the academic and cultural boycott of Israel, as well as for an economic boycott, to include Israeli products as well as the products of international corporations that are complicit in Israel's violations of international law. The BDS campaign has actually succeeded in many cases in convincing top international artists and bands not to perform in Israel, and in influencing international academia to boycott the Israeli academic institutions that are deeply implicated in planning, implementing, justifying and whitewashing Israel's crimes against the Palestinian people. BDS adopts a rights-based approach, emphasizing the three basic rights of the entire Palestinian people: ending the occupation (including the settlements); ending the system of racial discrimination (which fits the UN definition of apartheid); and implementing the right of return of the Palestinian refugees, who constitute the majority of the Palestinian people.[22]

The Palestinian Campaign for the Academic and Cultural Boycott of Israel (PACBI) has gained increasing support. Publically endorsing the Palestinian-led, global BDS movement, Roger Waters, the English musician, singer, songwriter and composer, asserted:

Where governments refuse to act people must, with whatever peaceful means are at their disposal. For me this means declaring an intention to stand in solidarity, not only with the people of Palestine but also with the many thousands of Israelis who disagree with their government's policies, by joining the campaign of Boycott, Divestment, and Sanctions against Israel.[23]

Articulating a simple yet compelling logic, an exceptional sense of moral responsibility, and a commitment to end complicity in the commission of injustice, Waters issued a plea to his colleagues in the music industry, and also to artists in other disciplines, to join the cultural boycott of Israel. He compared Israel's system of oppression of the Palestinian people to South Africa's apartheid regime, recalling how artists boycotted the latter, and its infamous Sun City resort, as a matter of moral duty. His move has effectively ushered in a new phase in the spread of BDS to millions across the world who had not previously heard of the budding rights-based movement.

Roger Waters is certainly neither the first nor the only prominent cultural figure to call for a cultural boycott of Israel. World renowned and bestselling authors, including John Berger, Alice Walker, Naomi Klein, Henning Mankell, and Iain Banks; prize-winning filmmakers, including Ken Loach, Mike Leigh, the Yes Men, and John Greyson; violinist Nigel Kennedy and classical guitarist John Williams; the Irish artists union, Aosdana; and Belgian dance sensations Anne

---

22 For more information, see http://www.bdsmovement.net.
23 *The Guardian*, Friday 11 March 2011.

Teresa De Keersmaeker and Alain Platel are all among the many famous cultural figures around the world who have endorsed one or another form of the Israel boycott in the cultural sphere. Hundreds of artists in Montreal, Canada, Ireland, South Africa and India have also formed artists-against-Israeli-apartheid type groups that have played a critical role in spreading the cultural boycott into the mainstream.

Yet Waters's endorsement of BDS carries special significance, given the combination of his eminence in the rock music world where he enjoys a mass fan base of millions, his inspiring courage in advocating BDS, and his unwavering commitment to speak truth to power in defending equal human rights for all humans.

Towards the end of March 2012, Roger Waters surprised leading international media outlets and millions around the world when he announced, at a press conference in Brazil, a groundbreaking social forum for Palestine to be held in Porto Alegre. With his typical modesty and charm, he said that he was honored to have been asked by the Palestinian BDS National Committee to announce an initiative, in cooperation with the Brazilian social movement and international civil society networks, to hold the World Social Forum Free Palestine in Porto Alegre, Brazil in November 2012. But he did not stop at that. He explained exactly why he considers himself part of the global BDS movement, going on to assert, "We will continue our call for an end to the Israeli occupation of Palestinian land, for the tearing down of The Walls of colonization and apartheid, for the creation of a Palestinian state with its capital in Jerusalem, for the granting of full and equal rights to the Arab-Palestinian citizens of Israel and for promoting the rights of Palestinian refugees to return to their homes as required by the Geneva convention, as stipulated in UN resolution 194, in 1949 and as restated by the International Court of Justice on the 9th of July 2004." [24]

---

24 Roger Waters, statement, Rio de Janeiro, March 28, 2012. Published on *The Electronic Intifada*, 03/29/2012.

This level of political awareness and unwavering commitment to Palestinian rights – both extremely rare among stars of the stature of Waters – was born out of Waters' history of advocating human rights around the world and his unique experience with the question of Palestine, first through his father's eyes and later through his own. "My conviction is born in the idea that all people deserve basic human rights," he reminds us. When he visited occupied Jerusalem and Bethlehem in 2006, he wrote: "Nothing could have prepared me for what I saw that day." He added:

In my view, the abhorrent and draconian control that Israel wields over the besieged Palestinians in Gaza and the Palestinians in the occupied West Bank (including East Jerusalem), coupled with its denial of the rights of refugees to return to their homes in Israel, demands that fair-minded people around the world support the Palestinians in their civil, nonviolent resistance. [25]

Kairos Palestine: A Moment of Truth also endorsed the BDS movement. Kairos Palestine was launched by Palestinian clergy and lay Christians in December 2009 as a word of faith, hope, and love spoken from the heart of Palestinian suffering. This organization calls on our leaders and policy-makers to find the way of justice and equality, and to realize that this way is the only path to genuine peace.

Churches around the world have also become much more vocal than ever before in support of Palestine. Methodist and Presbyterian churches put a lot of effort and spent hours on discussions to get a vote in their general assemblies on divestment from companies that support the occupation. Unfortunately, however, they failed to pass a resolution on divestment. However, they succeeded in facilitating a very strong educational process. They also succeeded in passing a vote to boycott products of the settlements, as did the Quakers in Britain.

Over and above these achievements, The Friends Fiduciary Corporation (FFC) voted to divest from Caterpillar Inc., the

---

25 Roger Waters, "Tear Down This Israeli Wall," *The Guardian*, March 11, 2011.

corporation that manufactures the bulldozers used by the Israeli armed forces for house demolitions. In addition, in June 2012 it was officially announced that pension fund giant TIAA-CREF (Teachers Insurance and Annuity Association – College Retirement Equities Fund) had removed Caterpillar, Inc. from its Social Choice Funds portfolio. Moreover, the renowned writer Alice Walker, author of The Color Purple, for which she won the National Book Award and the Pulitzer Prize, refused to allow the Israeli Ydiot Books to translate her book into Hebrew.

A recent voice came from the United Church of Canada when they voted on August 14, 2012 to boycott products of Israeli settlements. Peter Larson, Vice-President of the National Council on Canada-Arab Relations and chair of its Education Committee on Israel/Palestine, announced that the United Church had brought "a difficult issue back into the mainstream:"

The recent decision by an overwhelming majority of the nearly 400 delegates of United Church of Canada to support a boycott of goods from the illegal Israeli settlements in the West Bank was significant in four important ways:

First, because the Church has dared to approach this issue at all.

Second, because the decision was so overwhelming.

Third, because the Church's deliberate and thoughtful process was respectful of all and every opinion.

Fourth, because the discussion on Israel/Palestine now moves back to hundreds of United Church congregations across Canada.[26]

Larson wondered "how long it will be before such an informed discourse reaches the ultimate public policy forum: Parliament itself?" [27] We join him in wondering the same question about the American Congress.

What drew even more attention and controversy was a letter sent to the US Congress on October 5, 2012 by 15 prominent American Christian leaders. This letter stated: "As Christian leaders

26 Published on *Jewish Voice for Peace*, www.RabbisLetter.org, nd.
27 Ibid.

in the United States, it is our moral responsibility to question the continuation of unconditional U.S. financial assistance to the government of Israel, as continuing such aid will only serve to sustain the status quo and Israel's military occupation of the Palestinian territories." The letter also called on Congress to make military aid to Israel "contingent upon its government's compliance with applicable U.S. laws and policies." [28] Unfortunately, the Presiding Bishop of the Episcopal Church did not endorse the letter, and the Episcopal public policy director, Alexander Baumgarten, said that the request for congressional hearings was not in line with Episcopal policy. I have never heard of a church policy that contradicts the demand for human rights. After all did not our Lord come to preach good news to the poor, to proclaim freedom for the prisoners and recovery of sight for the blind, and to release the oppressed (Luke 4:16)? One would think that the Presiding Bishop would have raised her voice on behalf of the small, voiceless Palestinian community, and on behalf of its Bishop in Jerusalem, whose hands are tied because of the occupation.

As a result of this letter, Leslie Scanlon reported in the Presbyterian Outlook that "tensions are running high between Jewish groups and an alliance of mainline denominations." and that leaders of Jewish groups had canceled an upcoming meeting of an interfaith group. Leaders of Reformed and Conservative Jewish groups, the American Jewish Committee and other Jewish groups sent a letter on October 17, 2012, expressing their distress and saying they would not attend a planned meeting of the Christian-Jewish Roundtable, an interfaith discussion group formed in 2004.[29]

Rabbi Brant Rosen, writing in the Jewish Journal on October 24, 2012, observes, "Considering the vehemence of such a response, one might assume that the Christian leaders' letter was filled with outrageous and incendiary anti-Israel rhetoric. But in fact their letter

---

28   Reported by the Presbyterian News Service; full text of letter available online at http://www.pcusa.org/news/2012/10/5/religious-leaders-ask-congress-condition-israel-mi/

29   Presbyterian Outlook, October 19, 2012.

is a sensitively worded and faithful call supporting both Israelis and Palestinians in their desire to live in peace and well-being." Rabbi Rosen explains that there has long been an unwritten covenant between the Jewish establishment and Christian leaders when it comes to interfaith dialogue: "We can talk about any religious issues we like, but criticism of Israel's human rights violations is off limits." He goes on to explain why the Jewish establishment reacted so violently to a relatively balanced and religiously based call. By speaking their conscience, these Christian leaders had the audacity to break the unwritten covenant: "If you want to have a dialogue with us, leave Israel alone."

If that is the case, then those Jewish leaders who decided not to attend the roundtable meeting will not be missed. If interfaith dialogue is simply another tool used to shield Israel from accountability, then it will be a futile exercise. One would hope that interfaith dialogue would bring together the moral values of each faith so as to enhance understanding, promote peace, and encourage people to work for a better world for all. For unlike as in politics, in genuine interfaith dialogue there should be no double standard and no vested interests; otherwise it will end up being a cosmetic and hypocritical dialogue.

A similar reaction took place earlier when the Board of Deputies of British Jews pulled out of meetings in July 2012 with Lambeth Palace, the official residence of the archbishop of Canterbury, because the Anglican Church's highest legislative body had voted overwhelmingly to strengthen ties with the Ecumenical Accompaniment Program in Palestine and Israel (EAPPI). This program, an initiative of the World Council of Churches, "brings internationals to the West Bank to experience life under occupation. Ecumenical Accompaniers (EAs) provide protective presence to vulnerable communities, monitor and report human rights abuses and support Palestinians and Israelis working together for peace."[30]

---

30 See EAPPI website, http://www.eappi.org/

Once again, exposure of the truth is basically what worries the supporters of Israel.

In their collection, After Zionism, Antony Loewenstein and Ahmed Moor bring together essays—by Omar Barghouti, Diana Buttu, Jonathan Cook, Joseph Dana, Jeremiah Haber, Jeff Halper, Ghada Karmi, Saree Makdisi, John Mearsheimer, Ilan Pappe, Sara Roy and Phil Weiss—that explore the conflict between Zionism and the Palestinians and consider the possibilities of a one-state solution. As the description of the book states:

Time has run out for the two-state solution because of the unending and permanent Jewish colonization of Palestinian land. Although deep mistrust exists on both sides of the conflict, growing numbers of Palestinians and Israelis, Jews and Arabs are working together to forge a different, unified future. Progressive and realist ideas are at last gaining a foothold in the discourse, while those influenced by the colonial era have been discredited or abandoned. Whatever the political solution may be, Palestinian and Israeli lives are intertwined, enmeshed, irrevocably. [31]

Such voices, raised through books, articles, conferences, Witness visits, advocacy, and statements, have helped Palestinians a great deal. But we are at a stage that unless there is active defiance of this occupation, both on the local scene and on the international arena, there will be no chance of peace. Mrs. Eleanor Roosevelt once said: "It isn't enough to talk about peace. One must believe in it. And it isn't enough to believe in it. One must work at it." The Palestinian narrative needs to be continuously heard. But given the deadlock we are in, after all those long years of futile negotiations, perhaps it is time for a new *Intifada*.

---

31 http://www.saqibooks.co.uk/book/zionism/

Simply Reflecting

Those Were Not Normal Times

Living under a military occupation, I often find myself reflecting on what is going on around us, whether events or personal experiences. Even the Israeli soldier cooped up in a watch tower, guarding the military base near our house, inspires me when I catch him singing all alone or shouting at the slightest movement around him. Despite his being part of the occupation system, I must admit that I do occasionally feel sorry for him. I am sure he would love to spend the night with his family, especially during the miserable rainy days or during the hot months of the summer. After all, he is human. Tragically, the occupation is bound to demoralize those soldiers and destroy their humanity, just as it also demoralizes us and destroys our own humanity.

One of the casualties of military occupation is simply a normal life. In normal times in our country, when someone dies the funeral takes place within twenty-four hours, and an obituary is published in the local papers specifying the time of the funeral and the days on which the family will receive condolences. In normal times wedding cards are sent ahead of time, so one can plan to attend. In normal times many organizations have summer programs, camps for children and youth, and fun days. And in normal times people take a vacation from work every year.

But during the days of the *Intifada* specifically, times were not normal at all, and resisting the occupation seemed to be the only normal thing to do. To suppress the second *Intifada*, the occupying military forces imposed a general curfew during the summer of 2002, restricting people to their homes except for the limited hours allowed for some shopping. No matter how much one tried to plan, under curfew nothing seemed to work out. Under curfew, life was literally on hold. Under occupation, even our dreams are put on hold. A simple plan for a summer vacation, for instance, became an ordeal. Travel via the airport was not allowed for the residents of the West Bank and Gaza; travelers had to cross the Allenby Bridge to travel via Jordan. But crossing the bridge was practically "mission impossible" when people needed to spend two to three nights sleeping in Jericho before being able to cross. (All cars have to go through Jericho before crossing the bridge, and people often choose to sleep there in order to be first in line for the crossing the next day.) Travelling under such conditions is such an ordeal that one is almost better off staying home.

Because of the curfew, the Fun Day for the children of Ramallah planned by the Sakakini Cultural Centre during the summer of 2002 had to be rescheduled a number of times. Finally, an announcement was issued, simply stating that the program would take place on the first day the curfew was lifted. The Fun Day did finally take place, and there was a good turn out. The children were in dire need of fun in between closures, curfews and incursions. A friend of mine in Nablus called to say that after eight days of complete curfew the children defied orders and simply took to the streets, making percussion music with their spoons and empty plates to express their need for basic food.

Munir, the son of a friend of ours, died in Bethlehem during the curfew period. There was no announcement for the funeral because nobody knew when it would take place. The funeral was eventually held four days later. The family announced that they would receive condolences whenever the curfew was lifted. The funeral of Fatimah, an activist friend of ours, met the same fate in Ramallah around the same time.

Wedding invitations during those days had no specific date. Instead, an hour and a place would be specified for the first day the curfew was lifted. A friend of mine told me about a wedding in Ramallah which was supposed to take place at 12:00 noon on the day the curfew was lifted. Upon hearing that the curfew was going to be imposed again an hour earlier than originally scheduled, the wedding entourage rushed to the church. Of course, most of the guests could not make it on time, but what mattered really was to get the formalities over with before the curfew was imposed again at 1:00.

I remember that after attending a 10.00 am funeral service in Beit Jala, we were not yet out of the church before the flower stands were rushed in for the wedding that was to take place shortly after. The wedding ceremony had to finish before the curfew was imposed again at noon. The people called upon to attend both occasions must have hardly have had time to go home and change from mourning attire to something brighter for the wedding.

The invitation that summer to the wedding of Amal, the daughter of Emile and Hanan Ashrawi, was one of the last wedding invitations we received from Ramallah that had a specific date. The wedding did take place on schedule. But because of checkpoints and borders we could not go. I did manage to send them a gift with my friend Cedar, who happened to be in Jerusalem, and who lives in the same neighborhood in Ramallah. Little did I know that the vase I chose as a symbolic gift from the Palestinian Pottery Factory in Jerusalem was almost going to cost Amal, Cedar's daughter, her life. Amal had volunteered to deliver the gift once the curfew was lifted. Package in hand, she headed towards the Ashrawi residence. To her great surprise, there was a massive Israeli army tank blocking the Ashrawi residential entrance. She stepped off the pavement and walked towards the tank, intending to go around it into the house. To her horror, the tank gun swung around and pointed its gaping mouth at her. Apparently she looked suspicious with her mysterious package. She stood in the middle of the road, frozen with terror, searching for a human face to appear from this monster, anyone with whom she could communicate. But the tank was simply a faceless, terrorizing object. Out of nowhere a car honked, which made Amal jump out of her wits. It was the Ashrawis coming home; she handed them the gift and ran back home.

Under a military occupation, when life could never be absolutely normal, being caught in the wrong place at the wrong time could be disastrous.

On March 21, 2004, Rima Khoury was looking forward to celebrating Mothers' Day with her children. As a dedicated young mother she had never contemplated working outside the home, feeling strongly that motherhood was a career in itself. Bringing up David, George and Aline was a full time job for her.

Her 20-year-old son, George Khoury, always seemed to be in a race against time, as if fearing that he would not manage to complete whatever he had started. Little did he know that time would win the race. George did not realize, when he went out to go jogging on French Hill that Mother's Day, 2004, that he would not be coming back to his room to finish the work he had left on his desk. Before he went out, he gave specific instructions that no one should touch his papers or his computer. But George never came back home. He was shot dead while jogging, mistaken for an Israeli. He left so much undone.

Mothers' Day will never be the same for Rima. It will always be a memorial for that special day "celebrated" ironically at the cemetery. Thousands of people gathered from Jerusalem and the Galilee to pay tribute to George, one more victim of the Israeli Palestinian struggle.

Truly, the Israeli occupation has left little room for hope anymore. It breeds a desperate generation of young Palestinians who have nothing more to lose. It is not surprising that those young men will continue to struggle by all means possible, yet it is very difficult to justify such a killing. Why a single individual? Why a university student? And why in a public place where Israelis and Palestinians in this paradoxical land could easily be using the same path?

Ironically, it was a Palestinian family that tasted the suffering that day. The apology that appeared in the local papers will not bring life to George or return him to his parents. So unless this apology actually means a change of strategy in the resistance movement, the apology is meaningless, and George will be neither the first nor the last victim of such sporadic, futile acts. In fact, as early as 1974, in Ramallah, shortly before Christmas, Hanna Tams, wearing a hat that was unfamiliar in Palestinian society, was mistaken for an Israeli and shot dead. He left behind him a young widow with four girls and three boys, who turned into activists themselves when they grew up, spending years on the run or in Israeli jails after Sharon coveted their house in the Old City and confiscated it. Shehadeh Didis, the marketing manager of a drug store, was another victim during the second *Intifada*. He was driving through the West Bank on January 16, 2002 to deliver medicines. With his yellow license plates, he was mistaken for an Israeli and shot to death. The bereaved mother who had begged him not to go could not be consoled. Yet her faith eventually sustained her, especially since she had already offered one of her boys to the church as a priest.

Even if the killers thought that those young men were Israelis, shooting haphazardly at civilians, whoever they may be, is not going to change the course of the political scene. On the contrary, such shootings are most irresponsible. If activists are planning to liberate the land, then surely it is a tragedy if they are unable to come up with a more fruitful strategy. Whether through armed struggle or through non-violent resistance, a strategy for liberation should focus properly and act responsibly in order to achieve its goal. Otherwise the mistakes will be endless. And when Palestinians end up shooting Palestinians, the hurt will be greater still.

Never a Dull Moment

Not only can it never be a normal time under a military occupation; but there is never a dull moment either. There is always a new story or experience to report. As much as one tries to keep an appointment, to get to work on time, or to run an errand, there is never a guarantee that plans will work out.

When my husband Yousef needed to go to the hospital for some blood tests one morning in March 2004, we started fairly early lest we face any obstacles. One of the main checkpoints getting into Jerusalem was close to the bottom of the hill where we live. We had to go right from the road and then make a U-turn just before the checkpoint to go south towards Jerusalem. We had hardly arrived there when army personnel stopped us to check our IDs and the car license. Eventually we realized what the whole issue was about. Along with the army, staff from the Israeli television licensing department were checking for names of people who had not paid their TV license fees. We had never once received a bill for the license, nor any reminder for the last few years. I tried to tell them that, but Yousef was in no mood to argue, and ended up paying the amount of NIS2430 (equivalent to $550) by credit card. I realized how sick he must have been that morning, for he would never normally spare an opportunity to take on a fight where injustice was concerned. It is unbelievable what this military government thinks up to make life hell for us. We compared notes with many other people who went through the same ordeal. Apparently the officers at the checkpoint were picking on people who had fairly new cars, so that they could threaten confiscation should the car owners refuse to pay. But it turned out that our financial harassment was the least exciting of the day's events.

On that same day, our son Suhail, with his wife Rania and their new baby, hit the road to go to a doctor's appointment for the baby. They found the U turn closed by the army. It was not an issue of the TV license fees. The army was simply not allowing anybody to pass. They must have collected enough money from the TV licenses and so had to come up with another innovative plan of harassment. Suhail was determined to get through in time for the appointment, and kept arguing with the soldier, raising his voice loudly. Finally the barrier was removed and he passed through. However, our daughter Dina, who was taking her eight-year old son Faris to his afternoon music lesson, was not allowed to pass. She hoped that the sad look of disappointment on the child's face at the prospect of missing his drum lesson, which he loves, would soften the heart of the soldier. On the contrary, the soldier had a stone cold expression. And when Dina challenged him to look at the boy's face, and to look into his own heart and confront his own inhumanity, he became even harder and more determined to keep the barrier closed.

The worst experience was that of our niece Maha, who was on her way to pick up her child from the nursery. The soldier told her that she could not go through. She had begun reversing when she saw a car making the U turn, and decided to seize the opportunity and follow the car. The army stopped her and claimed that she was trying to run over the soldier. It was a very serious charge, but one that seemed simply absurd. The police intervened and took her to the station. It is at exactly such moments that a mobile phone comes in handy. Maha called home, and her brother-in-law went to her rescue, while another cousin picked up the child from the nursery. Of course, "all's well that ends well." But it was a hell of an experience for her, for no logical reason whatsoever.

But then, those were not normal times, and under a military occupation closing barriers for no reason is not a strange phenomenon. A week earlier a group of us from Sabeel were with Rev. Ateek in Ramallah for a meeting in preparation for the International Conference. On our way back we found the Qalandia checkpoint completely closed. There was no sign or announcement as to when it was going to open. For almost two hours we stood there, feeling so frustrated at our inability to do anything about this humiliation, and at the lack of concern for the human element. Rev. Ateek suggested we should start singing "We shall overcome." I did not think that this was the right kind of a song with the mob that was around. We could have done better with drums and some Arabic songs like "Biladi Biladi" (the national anthem). But then we might have stayed there overnight—we knew very well that any provocation on our part would probably cause the army not to open the barrier at all. In retrospect, I felt guilty that we acquiesced and waited peacefully like a herd of sheep. When we were eventually allowed to go through, it felt like being released from jail. And we were only there for two hours; I could not help but think of how the young men and women who have been languishing in Israeli jails for years must be feeling.

Yet all those experiences, no matter how infuriating, do not even begin to compare to the atrocities of the military occupation forces as they continue to raid the Palestinian Territories. The memory of Huda, a child found wandering in a daze during the shelling of their area in Gaza early in June 2006, searching for her family who had all been killed, continues to be a haunting scene. The Israeli atrocities and crimes do not surprise us anymore. But what continues to surprise us is that Israel is allowed to get away with those atrocities. The economic, scientific, and cultural international boycott of the Apartheid regime in South Africa was one of the most effective means to end that regime. Why is it being resisted regarding Israel?

When nothing is normal, anything can be absurd. I was at my sister's home in Ramallah for tea in honor of a Canadian friend of hers a week before Easter in March 2005. We had been told that the Israeli military were issuing permits to the Christians of Ramallah and Bethlehem to visit Jerusalem during the Holy Week. How magnanimous of the Occupation Authority, given that the week before they had refused entry to a woman from Bethany to deliver her baby at the hospital in Jerusalem; she ended up delivering it at the checkpoint. I invited the friend, who was keen on coming to

Jerusalem, and her husband to join us for lunch after her pilgrimage to Jerusalem. She eventually showed up without her husband. Although all through the year he had a permit to enter Jerusalem, it turned out that his regular permit was not valid for "Pesach."

Just as absurd was the experience of my grandchildren coming from Bethlehem with eggs from their uncle's little farm. The Easter season for the children is always connected with eggs, and with the joy of coloring them for the egg hunt. I still remember how excited we used to be as children when we would go into the chicken coop in Birzeit and pick fresh eggs. That day my grandchildren experienced that same joy, but not for long. Their joy was marred by the Bethlehem checkpoint.

They had gone to Bethlehem with their parents to celebrate Mothers' Day with their maternal grandmother; an occasion which is celebrated in Palestine and the Arab World on March 21 each year. They were so excited to get those fresh eggs, and were looking forward to the process of boiling them and coloring them to be ready for Easter morning that same week. But the order at the checkpoint was clear: "You cannot take those eggs into Jerusalem. You either keep them here or return them to Bethlehem." Well, the children were certainly not going to keep them "here." They were disappointed and scared, and had no intention of rewarding the soldiers with fresh eggs. Their aunt from Bethlehem picked up the eggs.

The rationale given, that no Palestinian products are allowed into Israel, is just as absurd, because it was very clear from the size of the package that those eggs were not going to be used for commercial purposes. Over and above this, according to international law East Jerusalem is not part of Israel. At the same time one cannot help but wonder why Israeli products are flooding the Palestinian market. Is this part of the concessions forced on the Palestinians in the Oslo Accords, the Paris Economic Agreement, or the Road Map?

But then, that is not all that we experienced at the Bethlehem checkpoint. Many years later, in the spring of 2012, after a lovely lunch in Bethlehem with some friends who live in Beit Sahour, we headed back home. As we were going through the checkpoint to be searched, we noticed with surprise that there were hardly any cars ahead of us. Well, we were in for a real surprise. After presenting our identity cards, we were requested to move to a large space full of parked cars. The passengers were outside of their cars. In front of every parking space there was a pipe to which the soldier connected a hose, which he then stuck into the cars. Whether he was pumping in or pumping out we could not tell. He ordered us out of the car. We refused, and my cousin who was driving explained to him that he had two women in the car who could not stand. His sister Laura and I had our canes with us to vouch for that, and my daughter Dina was squeezed between us in the back seat. The soldier would not listen. "Everybody out," he insisted, but we did not budge. Apparently the supervisor noticed that there was an argument going on, and came to check, and we were spared the new innovative "security" experiment.

Barriers

Despite those long years of occupation, it is not possible to get used to it or to feel that these are in any way normal times. Life under occupation has been a series of nightmarish surprises. So no wonder I thought it was too good to be true when I saw the checkpoint down the road from our house dismantled one spring day in 2009.

The first thought that came to my mind was that now I could drive straight through to the home of my friend, Cedar, or she could walk down on a sunny day and meet me on the main road so that we could go to Sabeel together. But my joy was soon to turn into shock and dismay when I realized that the checkpoint had been removed because the gate that was in the middle of the infamous Wall surrounding all the area adjacent to us, known as El Ram, had been terminally closed. This gate was the only outlet for people who found themselves imprisoned behind that Wall. So the new reality hit me right in the face. What I thought was a blessing ended up a disaster and a real curse for the population of around 28,000. Even the people "lucky enough" to be outside that Wall who normally did all their shopping, banking, and errands at El Ram had lost that access now. The office of Juzoor where my daughter works is approximately two blocks from home, but now she needs to go north via the Qalandia checkpoint before heading back south via El-Ram to the office. Eventually that office moved completely to Ramallah in June.

With no street names or street numbers in our area, our foreign guests always wonder how to tell the taxi driver to get them to a certain place. Giving directions without street names or numbers is almost like writing an essay. Ironically, the checkpoint was a helpful landmark. For example, one might say: take the first entrance after the supermarket, then the left turn after the traffic light. No, don't take the first turn, take the second one, just before the checkpoint. No, you don't pass the checkpoint ... etc.

One time we had houseguests from England, and to them the sign showing that there is a checkpoint ahead was the landmark to turn to the road that leads to our house. They rented a car to go to the Galilee for a couple of nights, and when they returned the checkpoint had been removed. Without this landmark, they almost missed the turn. Luckily they found their way due to the church at the corner of the street, another landmark that I had told them about when they were trying to find their way.

It reminded me of the story in our Arabic reading book in school about a fellow who hid his treasure in the field. He went to look for it, and could not find it. His friend asked him if he had marked the area. He replied that there was a cloud above it. Indeed, that checkpoint is like a February cloud that appears out of nowhere, and simply blocks the very-much-desired sunshine at that time.

In the meantime, work has been going since the fall of 2008 on the Shufat road for the light rail, despite the objections and boycott initiatives of the French company executing the work. So now the new barrier is not an 8-metre concrete wall, but a train that connects the Israeli settlements around Arab East Jerusalem with the Western part of the city, passing through Shufat and going all the way to the New Gate. The intruder is a locomotive that has imposed itself in our midst as though we do not exist.

Once again Israel has created a new reality on the ground at the expense of the Palestinian people. Ever since land became scarce in the heart of the city and building permits became next to impossible to obtain, the suburbs have been the only outlet for the development of residential and shopping areas. There was once a four-lane road connecting Shufat and Beit Hanina, busy northern suburbs of East Jerusalem, to the center of the city. Now there is a two-lane road divided by a railway on one of the busiest routes. Trying to get to the Sabeel office in Shufat from my home in Beit Hanina (about 6 km) with at least five traffic lights is already a nightmare, another station on what we call our contemporary "way of the cross."[32] But at this point the train has become part of the landscape. Indeed, it has become the means of transportation for many Palestinians living in Shufat. Ironic indeed: while Israel usurps the land of Palestinians it provides them at the same time with tempting facilities. I never thought I would see a Palestinian on that train. But for those who have never been here, and even for those who have and think they know the area, there is no way to envisage the new reality until one actually sees how history and geography are being created in the area.

Since 2009 the holy month of Ramadan has fallen during the summer months, which have been exceptionally hot, with the heat especially hard on those who were fasting. Almost every day during that month, around rush hour, when people were literally rushing to get home for the breaking of the fast, a military checkpoint was

---

32 A walk that Sabeel Liberation Theology Centre takes groups on to visit checkpoints, refugee camps, demolished homes, evicted families, the separation Wall, and the Palestinian usurped areas of pre-1948 Palestine.

put up on the main street between the end of Beit Hanina and the Qalandia checkpoint separating the occupied part of Jerusalem from the rest of the West Bank. Why this checkpoint, since all commuters have to pass through the Qalandia checkpoing anyway? No other reason could be justified for that "flying" checkpoint but mere SPITE. (Not that any of the other numerous checkpoints on the West Bank are justified, but the choice of the time and the place is, in this instance, glaring evidence of spite.) No wonder people have been so cynical about the peace talks, when a mere gesture void of spite cannot prevail even during holy days.

Gestures of Humanity

Yet amidst all that is happening a warm gesture sometimes comes along and reminds one that there is still some humanity around. I went to the Palestinian-run post office one summer morning to post a letter for my daughter. She wanted it to be sent "express," and I was rushing to get there before the place got crowded. Sure enough, I was one of the very first few. In summer it is no problem to get started early. It is so fresh and pleasant that by six one can easily be wide-awake. I was sure the coins in my bag were enough, and had no clue that the letter would cost close to a hundred shekels. I apologized to the postmaster, and told him that I would have to come back later, as I did not have enough money. I could not believe it when he told me that I could post the letter, and then come and pay later.

I sat reflecting in the car, remembering when we moved in 1964 from our Jerusalem apartment in the centre of the city to Beit Hanina, with no services or shops around. We had to drive all the way to Jerusalem to buy a loaf of bread. How we missed the little falafel stand near our house and the little nook that served delicious hummus with meat and pine seeds. Whenever we had company all we had to do was yell from the window and presto, all would be at our doorstep in a minute. Our rented apartment was also strategically situated in the heart of East Jerusalem, close to the National Hotel and Restaurant, so we could count on its hospitality when unexpected company dropped in. The hairdresser was next door and so was the movie house. And above all, our landlord was a pediatrician and his wife a professional nurse. With both children born in that flat I never needed to rush to a clinic, as our dear Dr. Majaj was always ready to run up the stairs when the children were sick. Indeed, we had a doctor in the house.

It seemed like we had moved to the wilderness, but because it was to our newly built home, we had something worthwhile to look forward to. The children had all the space and freedom to enjoy the wilderness and the wild flowers in the open fields around us. Another family had also moved that same summer to the street behind us. Up to this day my nice neighbor and I visit across the fence. Unfortunately, those open fields were filled up soon after the Israeli occupation in 1967 by a military installation surrounded with

Yousef and Abdallah with Dr. Majaj

barbed wires. Beit Hanina is now a booming suburb with all the services that the community needs, including a post office agency run by Palestinians. One hardly needs to go down to Jerusalem for any daily needs. Unfortunately, however, part of the old Beit Hanina has been closed, and its residents have no access to Jerusalem. Meanwhile, right in its midst a highway has been constructed to connect the Jewish settlements in the West Bank with the highway to Tel Aviv and the airport.

Despite the depressing situation, Yousef and I tried to lead a normal life, at least at home, and to enjoy our children and grandchildren. Until my father-in-law passed away in January 1990 at the age of almost 101, with his full mental and physical abilities intact, we were blessed by having four generations around. *Jiddo* (grandpa), as the children called him, was fit enough to carry his first great grandchild Omar into church for his baptismal, a wish he always hoped to realize. Omar was one year old when *Jiddo* passed away. Soon after his retirement in 2002 Yousef was diagnosed with stomach cancer, and our life style changed overnight. We needed a retreat to absorb all that we were about to face and how we were going to deal with it. So along with Yousef's brother, sister and their spouses we decided to spend a weekend in Tabgha near Tiberias, at a new pilgrim's house run by the German order Deutscher Verein Vom Heiligen Lande. We drove to that lovely spot for a retreat before Yousef was admitted to hospital, and we had a beautiful evening in Haifa and a joyful luncheon in Acre eating fish by the seaside.

No wonder Christ was inspired in the Galilee. The landscape and the sea must have been a perfect setting for his ministry. On Sunday the service was in the open air close to the sea, near a church known as the Church of the Seven Springs. An improvised altar was made out of Tiberias black stone, and the benches were logs of trees. A young German provided the music for German hymns on his guitar. In the midst of the service a cony jumped on the altar. One of the priests tried to shove it away, but the animal was persistent in its

Jiddo Anton with the grandchildren

Family retreat in Tabghah before Yousef's admission to hospital

attempts to be part of the service, until another priest used his habit to get rid of it amidst the giggles of worshippers. Another cony was roaming around, but must have realized there was no chance to get any closer, so it settled for another improvised stone table on the side where the chalice of wine and bread were laid out for communion.

In such a setting I could not but wonder what Christ would have done under such circumstances. Maybe during his time dozens of conies were around, and maybe they were just as much a part of the landscape. Maybe it is we who are intruding on the privacy of the cony and its partner in that wilderness. But the one thing I was sure of at the end of the service was that the Lord was listening as I prayed heartily to help Yousef and guard him in his long battle with cancer.

With little to occupy me besides reading, I had plenty of time to reflect as I accompanied Yousef on his chemotherapy sessions at the Sourasky Medical Centre in Tel Aviv, which was still known to many as Icholof hospital. When I saw that there were Arab doctors as well as patients in that Centre, I recalled the days in the 1940s when my mother was treated at a Haifa hospital by Arab and Jewish doctors and nurses. Will those days ever come back? Will the dream of a secular democratic state ever be realized? But most of all I could not help but wonder how such professional staff, who show so much humanity and do everything possible to save so many lives, be they Jews, Christians, or Muslims, could stand helpless against the Israeli military occupation which has claimed the lives of so many Palestinians and Israelis. And I could not help but wonder how they themselves could be part of the system that threatened harm to the same patients that they would have treated. I wondered again when I saw volunteers giving free meals to the families of patients who were anxiously waiting in the surgical section, or those who went around the wards on Shabat, the Jewish Sabbath, distributing cake and candles. Could these volunteers show the same compassion at checkpoints where hundreds of Palestinian men, women and children wait anxiously to pass?

We were at the hospital when a suicide attack took place on a bus in Tel Aviv. The injured were brought into the same hospital where we were. I saw many anxious faces. Listening to the women crying, my human and motherly instincts made me want to reach out to them. Of course, I knew a Palestinian was the last person they would want to see at that moment. But if I were an Israeli, it is probably Sharon who would be the last person I would want to see at such a time. I believe that his arrogant policy of maintaining this brutal occupation is the root cause of the suicide attacks. When will this madness stop? As long as there is a military occupation, there can be no security for anybody, and more innocent people will continue to be victims.

Intimidation is a common phenomenon all over the world. We watch bullies in the form of landlords intimidating tenants, employers intimidating employees, teachers intimidating students, and even parents intimidating their children. In general, the victims of intimidation are those who are weak and helpless, and those who do not have the guts to stand up for their rights or principles, because they hope to avoid trouble. We have the following saying in Arabic: "Stay away from evil and sing away." Very often when you share a story with your friends about the loss of your rights at work, or in regards to your property, nobody dares support you because of fear of the bully who was behind your loss. So people continue to be afraid, and shy away from confrontation.

Towards the end of May 2010 we saw a strange man in the neighborhood putting a fence around the plot near our home. When we asked him what he was doing, he claimed that he owned the land, and that he had bought it from its owners. We called the owner, who had bought the land at the same time as we did, in 1960, and she assured us that her husband, who had passed away, had never sold the land. When she appointed a lawyer to defend her case, a bully entered the lawyer's office and stabbed him. Luckily, he survived the stabbing, but he was intimidated into abandoning the case. However, with the encouragement of his colleagues, who promised to support him and stand by his side, he followed up on the case and proved that the bully had forged papers.

Almost at the same time, a travel agent in Jerusalem bought extra space for his offices, but some bullies who had coveted the same space intimidated him so much that he relinquished the sale and decided to "stay away from evil." After more than four decades of occupation, nothing is surprising any more.

Political intimidation is just as much of a phenomenon we are too familiar with in the Middle East. Under the guise of the so-called "peace process" much is permitted. Meanwhile, politicians and leaders cave in and relinquish their demands so as not to be accused of hindering that process. Even churches are being intimidated for taking moral stands. In their case it is not the peace process but the "interfaith dialogue" that is the target of the intimidation. I wonder how many will have the courage of the persistent widow, who kept taking her case to a mean judge. "But finally the judge said to himself, Even though I don't fear God or care about men, yet because this widow keeps bothering me, I will see that she gets justice" (Luke 18:4-5). Perhaps our problem as Palestinians is that we have not disturbed the international judge enough. If even the churches are not going to live up to the message of Jesus Christ, who was sent "to proclaim freedom for the prisoners and recovery of sight for the blind and to release the oppressed" (Luke 4:18), then most certainly bullies will continue to intimidate the meek, the poor and the oppressed, and lawlessness will eventually be the norm.

Part of my daily routine is to start the day by picking up the papers. We had subscribed to two papers, and it was very convenient when Yousef was alive, because each one of us settled with one. I could not keep up with both, so I drop off the second one at my son's home across the lane. However, I wonder why I even bother to get the paper. I watch and listen to the news every day, so there is nothing exciting about the headlines. But there is always news about so many atrocities taking place. The sight of children sitting on the rubble of their demolished homes, or news about confiscation of more land or closure of a road, aggravates my bright morning mood.

No matter what the pretext for these repressive measures, it is very clear that they are basically designed to make life unbearable for the Palestinians. Now I can understand why my sister-in-law stopped getting the paper, and why, when my blood pressures rises, my daughter urges me not to watch or read the news. But can we really do that? We are living in the midst of it all.

People in power seem to have a short memory—throughout history, oppressive governments have ended up learning the hard way, never heeding past experiences. We have seen and heard of empires falling and regimes tumbling, because the will of the oppressed people for liberation is always stronger in the long run. The sight of the Gaza people under siege, deprived of their basic needs, storming the borders and tearing down the fence should be a lesson. But can anybody teach Israel a lesson? It has graduated summa cum laude in democracy, human rights and international law.

Ever since 1967 we have watched again and again how disproportionate the Israeli Force's collective punishment of Palestinians has been. The punishment never fits the crime—that is, if resisting an occupying force is considered a crime. It is worthwhile noting that Gaza was exposed to shelling and targeted killing long before the people of Gaza even learned how to make rockets. What is significant to remember as well is that it was after the Gazan people had kept a period of calm for many months that Israel resumed its targeted assassinations. Perhaps one of the reasons for the Israeli unilateral withdrawal from Gaza in 2005 was to remove settlers from harm's way. Another reason was most likely the demographic threat that Palestinians pose to Israel.

Israel continued to besiege Gaza, and the area became the target of another wave of Palestinian ethnic cleansing. This phenomenon has been well articulated by the prominent Israeli academic Ilan Pappe in his latest book, *The Ethnic Cleansing of Palestine*. Another book that might touch the conscience of the Israelis and the international community is *Dark Hope: Working for Peace in Israel and Palestine*, by David Shulman. In a review of this book, Milton Viorst writes:

In opening his stunning memoir, David Shulman declares: I am an Israeli. I live in Jerusalem. I have a story, not yet finished, to tell. It is a very sad story, of a society gone astray with power, and of decent Israelis in despair over the failure of their efforts to save it from itself. The story, as Shulman says, is not yet over, but he asks whether its end is not already determined. Is tragedy inevitable? Can Israel right its course to achieve its once glowing promise as a refuge and as a nation? Shulman's memoir is not unique in raising these questions. Two recent books share his foreboding: Lords of the Land: The War Over Israel's Settlement in the Occupied Territories, 1967-2007, a careful work of scholarship by Idith Zertal and Akiva Eldar, and Toward an Open Tomb: The Crisis of Israeli Society, a stinging essay by Michel Warschawski. Shulman and Zertal are college professors, Eldar is a journalist, Warschawski is a peace activist. All are Israeli Jews. Whatever the stylistic differences of their books, they are equally unforgiving of Israel for placing its future in stark jeopardy.

None of these authors, it should be emphasized, is an apologist for Arabs. They do not deny that two peoples of vastly different cultures are engaged in a conflict of nationalisms, in which both sides have killed intemperately. All agree it is a conflict with too many victims, in both cultures. But these writers, good Israelis, are convinced Israel cannot resolve it by military superiority, much less by physical abuse.

[...]

Shulman tells of the uprooting by the settlers of thousands of olive trees, icons of the local culture and the chief source of income of the inhabitants. ... The settlers, he writes, "have stolen and desecrated not only olives, not only land, but the dignity that once belonged to Jewish books, the love I had for the ... Jewish God of my childhood, the musical Hebrew of my early poems. ... My own grandfather, a Jewish humanist of the old school, would never have believed it possible.... I know that I am seeing ... the prelude to the vast expulsion that these Jews are planning for these people {the Palestinians} all three million of them. Let no one say he did not know; let no one talk of vast historical forces, of wrongs piled on wrongs... let no one speak philosophy."

[...]

To explain why he and fellow activists, like the women of Machsom Watch[33], leave their warm homes to subject themselves to vituperation and sometimes personal peril, Shulman also conveys the thought that their concern is not just the Palestinians but Israel [34].

Will the wise words of those writers and academics fall on deaf ears? Or will Israel, as the stronger party, be magnanimous enough to put an end to all this brutality? Will it realize at long last that its security is dependent on granting the Palestinians their inalienable rights, their freedom and liberation from the yoke of occupation, an occupation that affects the stability of the whole region? The Holy Land, with Jerusalem, with its multi-religious and multiple cultures, in its midst, could be the jewel of the Middle East were this occupation lifted.

The Israeli Navy's attack in international waters on the Gaza Freedom Flotilla at the end of May 2010 is another of Israel's innovative and demonic ways of dealing with the tragic situation in Gaza. It was not the first time Israel had distorted facts and twisted information to appear as if it were itself the victim. The Israeli Navy surrounded the Flotilla, and commandos wearing full military gear landed on the ships from helicopters. Obviously, they were not a welcoming party to escort the ship to Gaza in order to deliver the humanitarian supplies the Flotilla was carrying. So why were the

---

33 Machsom Watch is a movement of Israeli women, peace activists from all sectors of Israeli society, who oppose the Israeli occupation and the denial of Palestinians' rights to move freely in their land. Since 2001 they have conducted daily observations of IDF checkpoints in the West Bank along the separation fence and in the seamline zone, on the main roads and on out-of-the-way dirt roads, as well as in the offices of the Civil Administration (DCOs) and in military courts.

34 "Milton Viorst on Israel's Tragic Predicament," Truthdig, February 1, 2008. http://www.truthdig.com/arts_culture/page4/20080201_milton_viorst_on_israels_tragic_predicament/

commandos there in the first place? And why did Israel impose a news blackout, preventing aid workers on board the ships from contacting the outside world?

We should not forget that the situation in Gaza has detoriarated as a result of the Israeli siege imposed on Gaza since 2006. The situation has been further exacerbated by Israel's Operation "Cast Lead," the military assault on Gaza from air and land that took place shortly before President Obama's inauguration ceremony in January 2009. Unfortunately, neither at that time nor later in November 2012, after the Israeli Operation "Pillar of Cloud," did we hear a clear condemnation of Israeli violence from the US Administration. Yet according to the Palestinian Centre for Human Rights, two-thirds of the Palestinians killed by Israeli Defense Forces (IDF) drones in that attack were civilians.

Dare we hope that this time may be a little different? I say "may be," because the ones who were hurt were not Americans, as in the case of the USS Liberty in 1967. [35]

Even the murder in broad daylight of US and British volunteers from the International Solidarity Movement (ISM) in Gaza, US citizen Rachel Corrie and British photographer Thomas Hurndal, did not move the US or British politicians to raise their voices and ask questions about what was happening on the ground. Rachel was crushed by an Israeli bulldozer on March 16, 2003, in full view of witnesses and photographers, as she tried to intervene in the demolition of a home in Gaza. Tom was shot in the head by an IDF sniper on April 11, 2003, and remained in a coma until he died on January 13, 2004. The shameful verdict at the Haifa court

35 The USS Liberty was an American intelligence ship that was attacked by the Israeli military on June 8, 1967, after 8 hours of aerial surveillance. According to the Findings of the Independent Commission of Inquiry, 30 or more sorties attacking the Liberty were flown by a minimum of 12 Israeli aircraft. During the attack all five American emergency radio channels were jammed. The Israeli aircraft dropped napalm canisters on the bridge of the Liberty, fired cannons and rockets causing 821 holes in the ship, machine-gunned the Liberty's firefighters and stretcher-bearers as they tried to save the ship and crew, and machine-gunned three of the Liberty's life rafts at close range. See http://www.ifamericansknew.org/us_ints/ul-commfindings.html

on the morning of August 28, 2012, exonerating Israel from any responsibility for the murder of Rachel Corrie, is another proof that Israel cannot face the truth, nor deal with it. And to add insult to injury, the court ruling further absolved the military from its responsibility for the killing of Rachel, stating that "The army had not been involved in demolishing houses, just clearing an area of places from which IDF had been attacked." However, Sergeant Hayb, who shot Hurndall, was convicted of manslaughter, obstruction of justice, giving false testimony, and inducing comrades in his unit to bear false Witness. On August 11, 2005, he was sentenced by a military court to eleven and a half years for manslaughter, of which he was to serve eight years in prison. But he only served a total of six and a half years in custody.

President Erdogan said it very courageously: "If everyone keeps silent, if all shut their eyes, if all turn their backs; we, as Turkey, we won't turn our back to Palestine, to the Palestinian people, to Gaza. We won't shut our eyes! We won't cease crying for Palestine!" Dare we hope that the international community would join Turkey in its efforts to put an end to this brutal occupation and to redress the grave injustice inflicted upon the Palestinians since 1948?

After all the declarations of Erdogan, I could not help but comment, "Et tu Brutus," when Turkish Airlines bowed to Israel's request to bar activists from flying into Israel for the Welcome to Palestine program in the summer of 2012. We expected more from Turkey. But we did not expect the European airlines to challenge the Israeli demand, because their cooperation fits perfectly with the political stand of the European countries. The scene at Ben Gurion airport was a shameful one, especially considering how Israel boasts of being the only democracy in the Middle East. Watching the violent force with which peaceful activists were met by Israeli security, one would think a nuclear war with Iran had started. Mr. Netanyahu advised those activists to go to Syria or Iran in solidarity with the oppressed people there. Little did he realize that demonstrations are being held inside Israel by his own people, at the entrance of "Bakum" in Tel Hashomer military base, in support of Israeli refusniks Noam Gur and Alon Gurman, who have refused to serve in the army of an occupying power. Those demonstrators are Israeli citizens, and live in the country. They do not need an airline ticket to express their solidarity.

The siege on Gaza not only created a humanitarian catastrophe for the people living there, but it created a new political reality. After Hamas won the elections in 2006 and formed a government, the US and the EU threatened to cut aid to the Palestinian Authority. Unfortunately, President Abbas caved in, and eventually Hamas established its government in Gaza. Thus began the rift between Hamas and Fateh, which jeopardized the Palestinian cause for justice.

How refreshing it was to hear Mr. Gordon Brown, the British Prime Minister, speaking in February 2010 on the 20th anniversary of the release of Mr. Nelson Mandela: *"His story reminds us that there is no corner of the earth so far away, no injustice so entrenched, no enemy so powerful that people of good conscience cannot campaign for, change and win."*

Indeed, how very true. And thanks to Mr. Brown for pointing that out, because it certainly gives us Palestinians some hope. After all, the root cause of the tragedy of Palestine began in Britain in 1917 with the Balfour Declaration, and with the British Mandate. It would seem to me that Britain should be the first country of conscience to redress the grave "injustice so entrenched" since 1948.

As I was going through my documents I found a Tony Blair file, which turned out to be empty. As I started to delete the file a flashing sign appeared on my computer saying, "cannot delete Tony Blair." Indeed, one cannot delete Tony Blair. When we thought there was a change in the British government he popped up again as the special envoy of the Quartet (the UN, European Union, USA, and Russia). Was Tony Blair supposed to resuscitate the body that has not given a sign of breath since its creation? Or was he supposed to give hope to the Palestinians in a hopeless situation? As Prime Minister he was in a much stronger position to enforce a settlement and bring about justice to the people who were victims of the British Mandate policy.

But my greatest surprise was to read in the English edition of the Israeli paper *Haaretz* on February 17, 2009 that former British Prime Minister Tony Blair would be one of the three laureates of the Dan David Prize for 2009, awarded annually by Tel Aviv University for the past, present and future. Blair was selected to receive the prize for the present, for what the judges described as "his exceptional leadership and steadfast determination in helping to engineer agreements and forge lasting solutions to areas in conflict."

Since Mr. Blair is the representative of the Quartet in the Middle East, one would assume that the prize would be given for his role in the M.E. conflict. But since his appointment the situation seems to have gone from bad to worse. I do not recall that he was able to bring about one agreement, let alone force Israel to abide by international law and comply with UN resolutions, unless I was on a trip to the moon during that great event. I am sure Jerusalem and its organizations can make better use of the allocated budget to maintain the offices of the Quartet and the salaries of its staff.

Fortunately, people of good conscience are already campaigning for Boycott, Divestment, and Sanctions against Israel. I hope that Britain will have the moral courage to set the record straight, and to support the efforts of the BDS movement, a campaign so similar to the one that brought down the Apartheid regime in South Africa, until the occupation comes to an end. Or will the rhetoric we heard from Mr. Brown on Nelson Mandela's anniversary of freedom simply wither into thin air? Will the "powerful enemy" continue to gloat over the fact that nobody will dare meddle with its policies? At this stage I find the words of Edmund Burke very appropriate: "*The only thing necessary for the triumph of evil is for good men to do nothing.*"

As an optimist by nature, my great hope is that some good men and women will do something, and that more will join them, so that together we may challenge evil and move ahead towards justice, liberation and healing.

Music

Amidst all the brutality and absurdities of the occupation, the arts, music and musicians have been our refuge and haven. During normal times as well, music was always part of our family life. As a student at Birzeit College in the early 1940s, I was privileged to have the renowned Palestinian musician Salvador Arnita as my piano teacher. At that time he was the Director of Music and organist at the YMCA in West Jerusalem. The school car would meet him in Ein Sinia, a little town down the hill from Birzeit, and the bus from Jerusalem would drop him off there on its way to Nablus. Unfortunately I eventually rebelled against those lessons, as I had no patience to practice, which did not please Mr. Arnita. Of course, I managed to find excuses; mainly that there were always other students practicing, so the school piano was continuously occupied. I was a little rebel in any case, but I could not use that excuse for long: the school bought another piano. I was so furious that I thought I would burn it with a match, but of course I burnt my fingers instead.

However, I was always fascinated by Mr. Arnita's playing of the pipe organ at the YMCA auditorium. We enjoyed so many concerts conducted by him in that auditoriam, as well as other activities. When Birzeit College held its last graduation ceremony at the YMCA auditorium in 1947, it was as if to bid farewell to that place that was so much the center of our early teenage days. Eventually that part of Jerusalem was occupied by Israel and denied to us.

As the years went by I realized how mistaken I was to abandon my piano lessons. That is why I was very strict with my children when they started their music lessons, especially when my son Suheil's clarinet teacher, Amin Nasser, and my musical sister, Rima, told me how talented he was.Very often I had to deprive him of privileges until he practiced enough. Like all children, he would accuse me of blackmailing him. He also reacted cynically when I tried to encourage him by saying that someday he would play in the Palestine Philharmonic Orchestra. Little did he know that he would, in fact, be the driving force behind the launch, on January 1, 2011, of the Palestine National Orchestra in Jerusalem. Earlier, in 1993, all three of them—Suheil, Amin, and Rima—along with Salwa Tabri and Nadia Mikhael Abboushi, had been founding members of the National Conservatory of Music, established under the auspices of Birzeit University. The Conservatory changed its name in September 2004 to the Edward Said National Conservatory of Music, ESNCM , as a tribute to the late Professor Edward Said for his intellectual and cultural contributions and his support of the Conservatory.

Unlike so many other parents who want their children to carry on in their footsteps and adopt their professions, Yousef was happy that Suhail opted for music rather than engineering. Yousef felt that Palestine already had an abundance of engineers, and that what was needed was artists to lift the spirits of our people. And that is exactly what Suhail has been doing as general director of the Edward Said National Conservatory of Music and through the various orchestras and ensembles of the Conservatory, as well as through his own music.

Yousef and I were so touched when Suhail dedicated one of his pieces to us during the Yabous Festival in the summer of 2002 at the Tombs of the Kings. The Yabous Cultural Center has been holding summer festivals in Jerusalem since 1996 with the aim of bringing

Suhail with his clarinet at the Yabous Festival at the Tombs of the Kings

life to the streets of East Jerusalem, which has been completely cut off from the rest of the Palestinian Territories since 1993. By 2011 Yabous had moved into its new premises after remodeling the old Al-Quds Cinema, now a beautiful center for cultural activities as well as a hall for movies.

On that specific evening Suhail was the star of the show as he accompanied the National Conservatory of Music group, "Karluma," on his Nai and Clarinet in nine pieces of his own composition. A number of these were inspired by the days he spent in Israeli jails during the first *Intifada*. These days are behind Suhail now, and I am so glad he found a beautiful and positive way to express his very difficult experience. As he put it, *"After the torture that I went through, I had two choices: either victory or defeat. And I realized it had nothing to do with how much I could physically bear, but with the way I was brought up, and that is why I was able to overcome. To my parents I dedicate victory."* As I listened, I could not control the tears of a proud mother. I could even detect a glitter of tears in Yousef's eyes. However, the tears of joy were mixed with tears of sadness for the many young people who are still languishing in Israeli jails. My joy was also mixed with sadness for my sister, brother, my brother's wife, and other family members and friends in Ramallah and Bethlehem who could not be with us on that special occasion because of the harsh measures of preventing West Bankers from entering Jerusalem.

On August 6, 2004, Fawanees, a musical composed and produced by Suhail, helped again to alleviate our morale and put us in a completely different mood and in a different world, making us forget for a short time that we are living under occupation. Sixty children were part of the cast for the musical, which was based on Ghassan Kanafani's story *The Little Lantern*. They were selected from schools around the area, and included my two granddaughters and a niece, as well as two girls from Rawdat El-Zuhur School.

A lot of effort went into the production. The script for the musical was adapted by Waseem Kurd, and was the first of its kind in Palestine. It was a relief for Suhail and his team (mainly the musical director, Fernando Nope, from Columbia, Hania Soudah, who was training the choir, and Edward Muallem, who was responsible for stage production) when they got the children and the orchestra on stage at last.

The opening performance was beautiful, and the show went on without a hitch. The audience expressed their appreciation for the program with endless clapping and a standing ovation. Everybody was smiling as they left the auditorium; the program really did help

A scene from the musical Fawanees

lift spirits. Little did they know how many tears were shed during rehearsals, and how many unforeseen obstacles the production team had faced. I remember that one of the saddest situations was when we had to call Suhail back from Germany, where he was working with the orchestra that was to accompany the musical. Yousef was in the last days of his battle with cancer, and we felt that Suhail would want to be by his bedside. It was sad that Yousef did not live long enough to attend the musical's grand opening.

Given all the preparations behind the scenes, I thought there should be another musical on the making of the musical itself. Taking into consideration the daily shuttle of the children across the checkpoints as they came from Bethlehem, Ramallah and Jerusalem, the German orchestra having problems with the Israeli authorities both upon entering the country and on the verge of returning, and the late hours of work at Turbo Design to get the printed pamphlets ready on time, all turned out beautifully. On the day of the final dress rehearsal, a day before the opening, when journalists and special guests were to be in attendance, out of nowhere water covered the place. Suhail did not know whether to cry, scream or simply laugh. He cancelled the final rehearsal and put all the effort into preparing the place for the opening night. It turned out that because the place was new, the fire system was being tested. That was all they needed! But all's well that ends well, and end well it did. Fawanees was performed eight times, and the Conservatory arranged transportation for students from far away areas to attend, so as to give them the opportunity to experience and enjoy this special musical event.

Nowadays, seeing children on their way to music lessons carrying their instruments has become a normal phenomenon in our society. It is, indeed, a blessing when children are given the opportunity to express themselves through music, drama and art, challenging all the obstacles, barriers and restrictions that stifle their every day life.

Over the last few years, The Palestine Youth Orchestra (PYO) has performed in Jordan, Lebanon, Germany, Greece and Italy. These young musicians are the best ambassadors for Palestine. The Palestine Strings, another ensemble of the ESNCM, were guests of the Mona and Bassem Hishmeh Foundation during their tour in the US in 2010. Towards the end of October 2012, one of the members of the PYO and the Palestine Strings, Omar Sa'ed, a Druze from Mghar in the Galilee who is still in high school, was summoned to do tests for serving in the Israeli army. As a conscientious objector, Omar wrote a letter to the military authorities announcing his refusal to serve in the army. His powerful statement was widely circulated, and his colleagues at the orchestra shared it through Facebook. (See Appendix IX.)

But the greatest achievement for the Palestine Strings was when they performed on August 8, 2013 for the BBC Promps at the Albert Hall in London with the renowned violinist, Nigel Kennedy and his group. My grand-daughter Rand, 13 was with the group on her cello and when they arrived home at 7:00 a.m. on the morning of the 10th of August she did not stop talking for two hours sharing that fantastic experience. She was also really excited to tell us that while they were boarding, the hostess at the British Airways recognized them as the Palestine Strings.

The hope that radiates with every cultural event was particularly present in the historic debut of the Palestinian National Orchestra—a dream come true. The Palestine National Orchestra was officially launched on December 31, 2010 in Ramallah and January 1, 2011 in Jerusalem under the slogan "Today an Orchestra and Tomorrow a State." The young soloist Mariam Tamari, daughter of renowned Palestinian artist Vladimir Tamari and his Japanese wife Kyoko, performed with the Orchestra as her first appearance in Palestine. Her beauty, presence and exquisite voice as she sang Mozarts Excultate Jubilate KV.165 added a special flavor to the whole concert. The performance included Gyorgy Ligeti's Concert Romanesc, Salvador Arnita's Allegretto and Beethoven's Symphony No.4 Op.60. Among the musicians, I was happy to see Nabih Boulos, first violinist, the grandson of my parents' good friends Nabih and Widad Boulos, as well as Charlie Bisharat, the nephew of a friend, Fred Bisharat, who along with others came from abroad to join the orchestra on this special occasion. A third performance took place in Haifa. This seemed to have been a unique experience for the Palestinian community there, as well as for some of the Palestinian musicians, whose families were originally from that part of Palestine and its surrounding area. It was particularly moving when the National Palestinian anthem was played before the performance. To the musicians it was a dream come true to be in the land of their forefathers. It is a dream denied to hundred thousands of Palestinians

The Palestine Strings in front of the British Parliament

The Debut of the Palestinan National Orchestra

in the *Shatat*, the diaspora, scattered all over the globe; a dream so many Palestinians have died for; but more than anything a dream we continue to live for. Through our art, music, folk dancing, literature, and culture we assert our presence and identity—and no occupation can deprive us of this. We are inspired by such glorious events to ignite the luminous future, in which music and art will embrace the dream for the right of return, liberation, justice and peace.

Appendices

Appendix I

The Spectator on Kamal, April 1973

The Spectator – 21 April 1973
Middle East
Death of a poet
Martin Short

On their raid into Beirut last week the Israelis stopped to fire ten or twelve shots into the mouth and jaw of one of their victims. This was more than just the gleeful act of vengeance it seems, for the man they did it to, Kamal Nasser, was not a gunman or a leader of gunmen. He was the spokesman for Al Fatah, the voice of the idea of Palestine. His broadcasts rammed home to his dispossessed fellow countrymen the belief that they had rights, that they could respect themselves: and that there were some people around who were going to get them back to their homeland.

A man of such wit, style and poetry must be far more infuriating for the Israelis than mere Kalashnikov-toting guerrillas. It is, of course, the very idea of Palestine which ultimately they have to assassinate. They can always kill ill-organised, freelance groups of Arab gunmen, but the notion of a Palestinian people and an articulated Palestinian consciousness is in the long term far more worrying for Israel. It is not just the ghost of Banquo at the Twenty-Fifth Anniversary Feast. In the Middle East the pen is not mightier than the sword — otherwise the Arabs would have won this conflict a long time ago — but Kamal Nasser, with all his swaggering bravura, has probably stoked up more trouble for Israel than all the arms in Arabia. His death should be seen as part of a pattern which includes last year's assassination of the PFLP ideologist, Ghassan Khanafani, and the news this Monday that the Israelis have arrested the editors of an Arab Jerusalem newspaper for a black-edged issue in mourning for the Beirut dead, which had not been submitted first to the Military Censor. Dangerous things, ideas.

The other thought provoked by Kamal Nasser's death is that he was a Christian, indeed an Anglican. The Arab cause in this ever more sickening Middle East conflict is often portrayed in the West as an aberration of the Moslem mind — to which no Christian could possibly subscribe — just the wild slavering of some schizophrenic Bedouin visionary. Such a character does exist in the patchwork of Arab politics, but for many centuries the Palestinians have been blessed, or cursed, by the missionary zeal of the West. And whether they are Latin Catholic, Greek Catholic, Greek Orthodox, Lutheran or Church of England, their experience and opinions of the conflict scarcely differ from those of their Moslem countryside.

So this son of Canterbury, Kamal Nasser, took up with the Palestine Liberation Organisation soon after the Israeli occupation of his home town in 1967. He was soon kicked over the Jordan, as was his brother-in-law — an Anglican priest but not a member of the PLO — who had spoken out robustly from the pulpit against the Israeli invader. And what have such men felt about the stance of their church princes on the Middle East conflict? Dismay and disillusion. The sight of the Archbishop of Canterbury himself, appearing to support terrorism in Southern Africa, while condemning it in the Palestinian arena, must have struck not only Arabs as an example of' double-think, even if the man genuinely sees any difference in the conflicts. More conscious, perhaps, of the long overdue need for reconciliation between Christians and Jews in Great Britain than of the feelings and emotions' of his lost sheep abroad, Ramsay has shown little sign that he even knows there are any Arab Anglicans. Last September he conducted an impressive service for the Israeli victims of the Munich affair.

Let us hope he manages now to say a tiny prayer for the soul of Kamal Butros Nasser.

Appendix II

Letter to Mr Moshe Shahal, Minister of Police

December 12, 1992

H.E. Mr Moshe Shahal
Minister of Police
Jerusalem

Hearing you lately on TV has encouraged me to write and let you know of the treatment I had at the Allenbly Bridge as I was crossing to Amman on Friday, November 27, 1992. As a Palestinian I know it is not a red carpet treatment that we get on the borders , but the unnecessary humiliation was absolutely not called for by any civilised measures. I am 59 years old and a grandmother.

I was at the bridge early enough to get on the first bus, but when my turn came to get my permit I was asked to wait. So after a long wait I was accompanied by two women-soldiers to the rooms where normally one is searched thoroughly on the way back from Jordan. Without any explanation and with very rude answers to any query that I made, I was very roughly and rudely asked to strip naked completely. And when I asked why was all that necessary, I am not a criminal, the only answer I got was "undress completely even this and that... and shut up". Again I was told to shut up when I asked why did they have to be so rude since I was asking them a question very politely. With the latest sophisticated technology controlling security these days it seems to me the whole process was unnecessary unless the intention was humiliation, and that is not humanly acceptable, and I am entitled to and explanation.

Thank you for your attention.

Yours sincerely,
Samia Khoury

Appendix III

Letter to President Bill Clinton

December 12, 1998
Mr. Bill Clinton
President of the United States of America

Dear Mr. President,

Welcome to the Holy Land. We know you have a busy schedule but we appeal to you to take a few minutes to read our letter and hopefully to help us resurrect our daughter's Identity Card from the tombs of the Israeli Ministry of Interior. After all, this is the Land of Resurrection. It is also a paradoxical Land because of the absurdity of the logic and narrative that prevails. By some mysterious way we can be present and absent at the same time. Yet we have not lost hope in justice and peace, and our faith has sustained us through the hard and long years of occupation.

Because we know you are genuinely interested in bringing about peace and justice in the Middle East, we are seizing the opportunity of your historic visit to the region to beg you to intervene and redress the grave injustice that has been inflicted upon our daughter Dina.

Dina was born in Jerusalem in 1961 and has always lived in Jerusalem. Even when she was studying nursing in London at the School of Florence Nightingale, she used to come home every three months. In 1984 she married an American citizen, Yousef Nasser, and they have three children all born in Jerusalem. As far as the Israeli Ministry of Interior is concerned, Dina and her three children ceased to exist when in reality we are still blessed with their presence around us in flesh and blood. When her youngest son was born in April 1995 she could not register him under her Identity Card, and was told she should register him under his father's. And when later on in February 1996 she went again to the Ministry of Interior to request the renewal of her travel document, both her travel document and her identity card were confiscated and never returned to her up to this day. In the meantime, an Israeli lawyer has taken on her case. After one year he regretted that he could not do anything because he was told that the right of residency in Jerusalem was a political issue. Dina is one of hundreds of Palestinian women who have been deprived of their right of residency in Jerusalem since the Oslo Accords, because their husbands are not from Jerusalem. If this is the outcome of Peace, we dread to think what it would be like in times of War.

Dina was refused reunification with her husband three times under the pretext that only a man can request reunification with his wife. Of course, a Jewish wife can reunify with her husband irrespective of where he comes from. And the status of a Jewish woman is never affected by the citizenship or residency of her husband. She may live outside Israel and obtain citizenship in two or three other countries without losing any of her rights either in Israel or in any of the other countries.

The US administration considers Israel to be the only democracy in the Middle East. How can democracy apply to one faith only when this Land has a population of many faiths? We ask you, dear sir, what democratic procedures can allow a woman to be deprived of her right of residency in the city of her birth, and where her life is centered? Dina is the Deputy Field Nursing Officer at the Headquarters of the United Nations Relief and Works Agency (UNRWA). She maintains a flat in Jerusalem and pays municipality tax (arnona). Yet when the municipality elections took place she discovered that she had no name. It is only in this paradoxical "Holy Land" that you can exist for tax purposes and cease to exist when you have rights!!!!

Please help us regain Dina's rights, and the rights of her children. And our best wishes to you and your family for a blessed Christmas, and a peaceful New Year.

Yours sincerely,
Yousef and Samia Khoury

Appendix IV

Acceptance Speech for the Citation Of Merit Award
The Alumni Association at Southwestern University

January 31, 2009

After I graduated from Southwestern 54 years ago, I never dreamed I would be on campus again, since traveling across the ocean during those days was not very common. However, when I met some loyal SU alumni, in Jerusalem in 1997, notably Billy Elmore and her husband Joe, the Adams, and the Shaws whose relatives were also SU alumni, I realized the ocean was not so wide after all, and my interest was kindled for seeing Southwestern again. And when I did return for homecomings in 1998 and 2004, I found this wonderfully new, virtually born-again campus.

I am sorry my cousin Diana who graduated at the same time with me and joined me on the last two homecomings, is not with us on this occasion because she could not leave her husband. I have been staying with her before coming here and reminiscing about our good old Southwestern days. My years at Southwestern are now fond memories. Some inspirational, some embarrassing, and some quite humorous, especially the times when my middle-eastern accent and idiomatic style of speaking attempted to interface with Texas talk. I was neither understood, nor could understand. (Bug killer, marriage of different sects, Dad gum it.)

Yes, all those memories are now treasures in my mind.

Today's event came as a great surprise to me and I am truly humbled and very grateful for this recognition. It makes me feel all the more fortunate to have had the opportunity to work as a community volunteer in support of education and social work and action in Palestine. So I feel that all the institutions and organizations that provided me with that opportunity deserve this award as well. Birzeit University as it was developing from a Junior College to a University, and the first in Palestine; the YWCA with its new challenges following the occupation of the Palestinians Territories in 1967; Rawdat El-Zuhur school, a unique experience of transforming a home for destitute girls to a formal coeducational elementary school with emphasis on quality education and moral values; and Sabeel Ecumenical Liberation Theology, as it works through non-violence for justice, peace, and reconciliation.

Of course I owe a lot to Southwestern University itself for providing me with the education, and skills that proved to be helpful in my career as an administrator and community volunteer. It was such a pleasure to see some of my teachers in one of the previous homecomings, especially Dr. Steelman and Mrs. Lundblad. Sadly they are both gone now. Of course I am specially sad also that my late husband Yousef did not share with me this day. He was always supportive and proud of my work. And he always enjoyed telling our friends what the YWCA stands for "Your Wife Constantly Away. Thanks to my daughter Dina who encouraged me to make this trip and has been taking care of me along the way.

However, I came for this event with a heavy heart as the brutal onslaught on my people in Gaza was going on. I am relieved that this nightmare is over at the moment, but that does not mean the problem has been solved. Had the United Nations lived up to its responsibilities and reversed the occupation of the Palestinian Territories soon after it took place in 1967, and insisted that Israel comply with UN resolutions, the region would have been spared so much suffering and the loss of many lives, Palestinian as well as Israeli.

Despite the illogic of the Israeli narrative that it has the right to defend itself, we have not lost hope. Indeed Israel would have the right to defend itself if it were not occupying and oppressing another nation. Shministim, the movement of Israeli conscientious objectors is one of the signs of hope. Those young men and women would rather spend time in jail than lose their humanity by serving in an army of an occupying force.

I have been in the USA for the last three weeks and found many Americans with a heavy heart as well, because of the deteriorating economic situation and the futility of the Iraqi war and the loss of so many lives and the loss of many jobs; increasing by the day. However you still need to count your blessings comparing to so many people around the world. But it is truly sad that as a genuinely good society, you end up being the victim of unethical policies of those in power, who are capable of limiting knowledge and subverting truth. I hope

Southwestern University, as an institution in the forefront of education, will continue to empower its students with the will to search for truth and to speak out against abusive power. I want to seize this opportunity to present the University library with two books. The Ethnic Cleansing of Palestine, by Ilan Papee, an Israeli historian, and A Palestinian Cry for Reconciliation by Rev. Dr. Naim Ateek, an Anglican Minister and Director of Sabeel.

We would like to see the change that President Obama promised as another sign of hope. I watched with awe the inauguration ceremony, and listened carefully to the speech of the president. I am sure all of you watching and listening on that day, were proud to have elected a president with stature and vision worthy of your country as a super power. You have come a long way. I still remember when I was in Texas in the early fifties, the black people had to sit in the back seats of the buses, and now you have a black American leading the country. As he focused on justice, I hope he will live up to the expectation of everybody and will genuinely work for the change that is needed to bring about justice, peace, liberty and dignity to the peoples of the torn countries around the world. A world that has become too small for each, not to care for the other.

At the Stanford University Memorial Church last Sunday, the interfaith service ended with this meaningful responsive reading.

"We are tied together in a single garment of destiny
We are caught in a network of mutuality
And I can never be who I ought to be
Until you are who you ought to be"

Once again I want to express my thanks to Southwestern University and the Alumni Association and to all of you who are here on this occasion. I know this was a great effort on your behalf, so I will always remember that it is your presence that made my day very meaningful.

Thank you very much.

Appendix V

Letter to President Yasser Arafat

December 2000
Dear President Arafat:

I am one of many women who have had their share of suffering and struggling under the Israeli occupation. Our hopes for peace were so high when the Madrid talks started, until we realized that with the Oslo Accords we were all taken for a ride. Every item in those accords needed another agreement for its interpretation and implementation.

Please Mr. Arafat, do no allow yourself to fall into another trap "Oslo Style" as you are being squeezed into signing an agreement that does not meet the minimum of the rights of the Palestinians and their aspirations.

The Al-Aqsa *Intifada* has said it clearly and loudly with the blood of our young martyrs: Enough is enough. No more negotiations until a complete withdrawal to the 1967 borders takes place, and the United Nations resolutions are implemented.

It is ironical that the president of the USA is dictating the rules of the game, when it is the US administration that has allowed Israel to get away with its non-compliance of UN resolutions. The prisoners who were supposed to be released with the signing of Oslo have been forgotten, and the settlements, "supposedly illegal" according to the international community, have grown to an enormous size while the "so much longed for lasting peace" has become a lasting process.

For the sake of peace you have taken a courageous step Mr. Arafat, and the Palestinians have already made a big concession by accepting to establish their state only in the Territories occupied in 1967. So it has to be all of the Territories. These percentages that are being offered are a way of making the Palestinian state an impossibility.

The Palestinian people will respect you and stand behind you when you stick firmly to the complete withdrawal from the occupied territories, the dismantling of the settlements, and the right of return for the refugees.

If Israel is really keen on peace let us see what compromises it is willing to come up with. But from what we see on the ground, I think Israel is scared of peace, because   it cannot be at peace with its own self. It cannot deal with all the internal problems of Israel; it needs a common enemy to hold the people of the state of Israel together. So hold on Mr. Arafat, you have a just cause on your side. But if you lose your credibility and your dignity we will all lose our case.

May the New Year launch the dawn of an era of peace for Palestine and the whole region.

Respectfully
Samia Khoury

Appendix VI

Ode to Security

In thy name O Security
Israel violates human rights with impunity
And turns the UN to an absolute mockery

Who dares challenge Israel's "democracy"
In the midst of an Arab World "autocracy"

Irrespective of Palestinian inalienable rights
With money and power Israel manipulates the tides

In thy name O Security
Israel resorts to arbitrary arrests and extra judicial killing
To confiscating land, razing groves and house demolishing

It determines who comes and goes for the Christmas celebration
Even Bethlehem like the day Christ was born is under occupation

As victims of racism, Israelis do as they please
Neither East nor West, do they need to appease

In thy name O Security
Israel's judicial system has become absolutely impotent
Since all Palestinians are guilty until proven innocent

For family reunification requests Israel has secret files
Not even lawyers can see them and refute the lies

That is why Israeli Judges have really nothing to say
But to reject every application with an absolute nay

In thy name O Security
We are all victims because you continue to be a priority
Occupation breeds hatred and is no guarantee for security
Despite the injustice of 48 we've accepted your borders
Ending occupation guarantees peace with your neighbors
Maybe it is time for your leaders and ours to realize
That without us Women no justice or peace can materialize

Appendix VII

Welcome Address at
Sabeel 1st International Conference

Faith and the *Intifada*

In the Holy Land, the cradle of the three monotheistic faiths, it is only natural that theology and religion should be at the center of our lives. At the same time, we have been struggling for liberation in our troubled land since time immemorial. But for us this is the first time that liberation and theology have come together on the same platform.

Religion has played a major role in the struggle of the indigenous people of this land. In the name of religion wars have been waged and under the pretext of religion violations of human rights continue to be justified. Religion has been used, abused, misinterpreted, and misunderstood. So much has been done in the name of God that His image has become distorted, so much so that we find ourselves struggling to hold on to our faith, or putting it aside. As Palestinian Christians we often feel embarrassed by our faith, because it is related so closely to the faith of our oppressors and their supporters.

The Christian faith, which we so proudly offered to the whole world as single unit, has often come back to us fragmented and in the form of religious colonization. It has been used to justify the many injustices inflicted upon us. And to add insult to injury we are always asked how and when we were converted to Christianity. We have always been Christians; but in our struggle for liberation we are together as Palestinians, Christians, and Muslims alike. There is a mentality of colonization and occupation that has tried to split our people on the basis of religion. Why do the security police at the bridge (the Allenby Bridge, the border checkpoint between Jordan and the occupied West Bank) ask me whether I am Christian or Muslim? What does that have to do with his obsession with security other than to create confusion and mistrust amongst us Palestinians? Luckily most of us are aware of this ploy.

Yet as Christians we cannot help but wonder: could all this suffering be blessed by the same God whom we know to be the God of love, peace, and hope? How does this faith relate to all the injustice that surrounds us? Can we truly turn the other cheek or love our enemy in this situation? What does Christian love even mean? To be submissive and to succumb to the forces that dehumanize us or to be angry, rebel, and do so something about it? I suppose if we were true Christians our faith would help us find the right answers, but we are not Christians by faith alone. Faith without action is dead. It is our deeds and our work with the poor, the oppressed, and the marginalized that will determine, whether we are true Christians.

This Conference is held at a time when the Palestinian-Israeli conflict is at a crossroads. We had hoped that the peace plan offered by the Palestinian National Council (PNC) on November 15, 1988 in Algiers would have been welcomed by the Israeli government. Since the establishment of the state of Israel in 1948 it has sought peace but claimed there was no one to talk to about peace. Now that there is a party to talk to, it has become clear that peace is not really on the agenda of the Israeli government at all. In spite of the concessions made by the PNC for the sake of peace and an end to suffering, the Israeli government has completely ignored the Palestinian peace plan and instead came up with its own initiative, the so-called election plan, a plan that seems to be leading nowhere. The prime minister who initiated this plan has no intention of negotiating with the Palestinians, most specifically the PLO which is our representative, which means no peace, as peace has to be negotiated between enemies.

As the *Intifada* goes into its third year, it has become increasingly clear that it has helped the Palestinians regain their dignity, and that the iron-fist policy of the military has failed to deter our young men and women from struggling and resisting occupation, a right of all people living under occupation. The prime minister's intransigence was demonstrated by his willingness to see the government collapse rather than making concessions and accepting the new reality that the Palestinians are his only negotiating partner for peace. He will have to answer to many Israeli parents whose young sons are becoming dehumanized and demoralized as they continue to play the role of occupiers and oppressors against all Jewish ethical and religious values.

"What doth the Lord require of thee but to do justly, to love mercy and walk humbly with thy God?"

We could not have chosen a better place than Tantur for a conference on liberation theology – midway between Bethlehem and Jerusalem, midway between the birthplace of our Lord Jesus Christ and the place of crucifixion and resurrection. May the spirit of incarnation and sacrifice, and the hope of the resurrection guide us in our deliberations.

Appendix VIII

Letter to President Obama

January 22, 2009
Mr. Barack H. Obama
The President of the USA
The White House
Washington, DC

Dear Mr. President:

I watched with awe and great respect your inauguration ceremony while I was visiting the USA. You were indeed an inspiration and a source of hope not only for the Americans but for me as a Palestinian, especially when you focused on the issue of justice. An issue which was also stressed in the sermon of Rev. Sharon Watkins during the National Service, the day after your inauguration. At last, I thought that the USA as a super power, and its good and genuine people deserve a leader of your intelligence and stature.

But somehow, Mr. President I was rather disappointed when you spoke after the announcement of the appointment of Senator Mitchell as a special envoy to the Middle East. You highlighted your commitment to the security of Israel without any reference to the word "justice." The grave injustice that was inflicted on the Palestinians upon the establishment of the state of Israel in 1948 and the occupation of the rest of the Palestinian Territories in 1967 is at the core of the Middle East conflict. So without justice, and peace no security can be granted to Israel or the whole region. In fact without the justice that was granted to your people in the aftermath of the civil rights movement, you would not be where you are Mr. President. So my heartiest congratulations to you Mr. President. The world is looking forward to that great change under your leadership.

So please do not let us all lose the spark of hope that was rekindled with your inauguration speech, and let justice be at the back bone of your domestic as well as foreign policy, especially for us Palestinians who had lost hope when Israel failed to withdraw from the occupied territories in compliance with UN resolution 242, and after the Oslo peace accords withered in thin air despite all the futile negotiations. Had the injustice inflicted on the Palestinians been redressed without delay there would have been no reason for Hamas to surface and to resort to arms struggle twenty years after the occupation. Surely Israel has the right to defend itself, but not when it is occupying and oppressing other people. In your speech this morning Mr. President you did not even allude to the occupation, and you put the occupier and the occupied on the same level. You are a well learned and well informed leader, so you certainly are aware that the Palestinians did accept to establish their state on only 22% of historic Palestine. The Arab initiative which you referred to in your speech is based on that offer as well. It is up to Israel now to prove that it is genuinely serious about peace.

So if you are truly committed to the security of Israel Mr. President, please do help Israel end its occupation of the Palestinian Territories. You have enough resolutions, peace agreements, and initiatives for Mr. Mitchell to work with, which could cut down the time and expense of another American shuttle diplomacy. Then you Mr. President, the secretary of state and Mr. Mitchell will go down in history for ushering a new era of justice, peace, and security for both the Israelis and Palestinians.

Respectfully yours,
Samia Khoury
A Concerned Palestinian Mother

Appendix IX

Letter of Omar Sa'ed refusing army service

Omar Sa'ed from Mghar in the Galilee, a member of the Youth orchestra of the Edward Said National Conservatory of Music refuses to serve in the Israeli military forces. He writes the following:

I received a summons to present myself at the recruitment offices on October 31, 2012 so as to go through the regular tests needed for the army service which is compulsory for the Druz community. But I wish to make the following statement:

I refuse to go through those tests because I completely oppose the compulsory army service for my people of the Druz community.

I refuse because I am a man of peace, and abhor violence in all its forms and believe that the military establishment is the optimum of physical and psychological violence. Ever since I received the summons I feel my life has been toppled upside down. I feel nervous and unable to focus. I remembered the thousands of harsh images and could not see myself in the military uniform and taking part in oppressing my own people, the Palestinians, or fighting my Arab brothers. In fact I declare myself as a conscientious objector and refuse to serve in any army.

I abhor oppression and oppose occupation, I detest any form of fanaticism or suppression of freedom, and I hate whoever arrests children, women and elderly men.

I am a musician and play the "viola" and I have friends, musicians from Ramallah, Jericho, Jerusalem, Hebron, Nablus, Jenin, Shafa'amr, Eilaboun, Rome, Athens, Amman, Beirut, Damascus, Oslo, and we all play for humanity and peace. Our only weapon is our musical instruments, and we shall not carry any other weapon.

I belong to a community that has been subjected to a grave injustice by an oppressive law. How can we fight against our own relatives in Palestine, Syria, Jordan and Lebanon? How can I carry arms against my brothers and my own people in Palestine? How can I be soldier at the Qalandia check point or at any other barrier when I have experienced the oppression of barriers?

How can I prevent people from Ramallah visiting their city, Jerusalem? How can I guard the separation wall?

How can I be the jailer of my own people when I know that most of them are prisoners of war and seekers of justice and freedom?

I play for joy, freedom, and a just peace, with an end to the settlements and the military occupation, and the release of all prisoners, and the return of the refugees. I play for the establishment of a Palestinian State with Al-Quds as its capital.

Many of our Druz men served in the Israeli army according to the compulsory law of service. But what did we get out of this? We are discriminated against on all levels. Our villages are the poorest, our land has been confiscated, there is no urban planning or industrial areas. The ratio of university graduates from our villages is the lowest in the area, and the unemployment ratio is the highest. That compulsory law has distanced and isolated us from our Arab community.

This year I will graduate from high school and I am hoping to be able to resume my university education. I am sure the military will try to bar me from realizing my humane ambition but I declare it loud and clear: I am Omar Zahr Ed-Deen Mohamed Sa'ed and will not be fuel for your arms or a soldier in your army.

Omar Sa'ed